SPEAK YOUR
PEACE

SPEAK YOUR PEACE

What the BIBLE Says about LOVING OUR ENEMIES

Ronald J. Sider

HERALD PRESS

Harrisonburg, Virginia

Herald Press
PO Box 866, Harrisonburg, Virginia 22803
www.HeraldPress.com

Library of Congress Cataloging-in-Publication Data
Names: Sider, Ronald J., author.
Title: Speak your peace : what the Bible says about loving our enemies / Ronald J. Sider.
Other titles: If Jesus is Lord
Description: Harrisonburg : Herald Press, 2020. | Previously published as:
    If Jesus is Lord. 2019. | Includes bibliographical references. | Summary: "A biblical
    case for nonviolence from one of the preeminent Christian leaders"—Provided
    by publisher.
Identifiers: LCCN 2019022437 | ISBN 9781513806259 (paperback) | ISBN
    9781513806266 (hardcover) | ISBN 9781513806273 (ebook)
Subjects: LCSH: Love—Religious aspects—Christianity. | Nonviolence—Religious
    aspects—Christianity. | Violence—Religious aspects—Christianity. | Jesus Christ
    —Example.
Classification: LCC BV4639 .S527 2019 | DDC 241/.697--dc23
LC record available at https://lccn.loc.gov/2019022437

Speak Your Peace is the trade edition of Ronald J. Sider, *If Jesus Is Lord: Loving Enemies in an Age of Violence* (Ada, MI: Baker Academic, 2019).

All scripture quotations, unless otherwise indicated, are taken from the *Holy Bible, New International Version*®, NIV®. Copyright ©1973, 1978, 1984, 2011 by Biblica, Inc.™ Used by permission of Zondervan. All rights reserved worldwide. www.zondervan.com The "NIV" and "New International Version" are trademarks registered in the United States Patent and Trademark Office by Biblica, Inc.™

Scripture quotations marked (NRSV) are taken from the *New Revised Standard Version Bible*, copyright © 1989, Division of Christian Education of the National Council of the Churches of Christ in the United States of America. Used by permission. All rights reserved.

Scripture quotations marked (TNIV) are taken from the *Holy Bible, Today's New International Version*®. Copyright © 2001, 2005 by Biblica®. Used by permission of Biblica®. All rights reserved worldwide.

Scripture quotations marked (KJV) are taken from the *King James Version of the Bible*.

SPEAK YOUR PEACE
© 2020 by Herald Press, Harrisonburg, Virginia 22803. 800-245-7894.
All rights reserved.
Library of Congress Control Number: 2019022437
International Standard Book Number: 978-1-5138-0625-9 (paperback);
    978-1-5138-0626-6 (hardcover); 978-1-5138-0627-3 (ebook)
Printed in United States of America
Design by Merrill Miller
Cover image adapted from Michael Powers/Getty Images

24 23 22 21 20   10 9 8 7 6 5 4 3 2 1

CONTENTS

Acknowledgments

THIS BOOK OWES a huge debt to such a vast number of people (a few of whom I remember; many more I forget; and the overwhelming majority I never knew) that I can only mention a tiny fraction as a way to say thanks to them all.

I acknowledge with deep appreciation the Anabaptist tradition in which I grew up and still live. The courageous and often costly witness to nonviolence of innumerable Anabaptists over five hundred years has shaped my life in more ways than I understand. My devout mother and father, Ida and James Sider, modeled peace in the family. My Brethren in Christ bishop, Bishop E. J. Swalm (one of my early heroes), lived his refusal to kill by going to jail in World War I.

I am grateful for the invitation (to me, then a *young* person) to give the Bible lectures at the New Call to Peacemaking (1978), sponsored by the Quakers, Mennonites, and Church of the Brethren. Those lectures resulted in *Christ and Violence*, my first small book on the topic of whether Jesus ever wants his followers to kill.

I have been blessed with good friends on the journey. Peace advocate John Stoner has been a good friend for almost fifty years. Richard Taylor, another decades-long friend and peace activist, coauthored a book with me on peace in a nuclear age.

To Merold and Carol Westphal (good friends from graduate school days), who vigorously insisted that this stubbornly proud person needed to agree to his wife's request for marriage counseling to save our marriage, I will be forever grateful. (I actually stopped to talk with them about our troubled marriage on the way home from delivering the peace lectures in 1978!)

To my darling wife of fifty-eight years, Arbutus Lichti Sider (who was right in 1978 that we needed marriage counseling!): I can only say a thank you from all my heart for walking faithfully with me in the hard period of painful struggle and also in the many decades of joy and peace before and after that time. You have been God's best gift to me after God's incarnate Son.

Three of my students at Palmer Seminary of Eastern University—Ben Pitzen, Joshua Carson, and Merrick Korach—provided invaluable help as they typed and retyped the manuscript.

This book is a much shorter, more popular version of *If Jesus Is Lord: Loving Enemies in an Age of Violence* (Baker Academic, 2019). In the vast number of footnotes in that much larger book, I acknowledge the large number of scholars and activists who have helped shape my thinking on peacemaking. When this book is used for Sunday school classes and other study groups, leaders will find it helpful to study the greater detail and numerous citations in that longer book.

With sadness and dismay, I also acknowledge that John Howard Yoder's writings have been important in my thinking. I appreciate the way his incisive ethics and theology have been widely influential on the topic of this book. I am also deeply saddened that the most brilliant theologian and ethicist in Mennonite history harmed so many women and disgraced himself with despicable sexual abuse and power abuse.[1] And I am dismayed that Yoder stubbornly resisted and refused counsel and correction, contradicting his own theology on communal discernment for many years. I understand why many people believe that Yoder's inexcusable, sinful sexual misconduct over decades means that we should no longer read his works. I have chosen to continue to learn selectively from Yoder, even as I grieve his atrocious failure.

Finally, I want to thank all the people around the world who, in both public and private dialogue, sharpened and deepened my understanding of both the just war and pacifist strands of Christian thought. All serious Christians wrestle with the question, "Does Jesus want his disciples to sometimes kill for the sake of peace and justice?" After more than six decades of adult wrestling with that question, I offer this book as my best answer.

1

The Central Questions

DOES JESUS EVER want his followers to kill? Should Christians ever use violence in order to resist evil and promote peace and justice? When Jesus commanded his disciples to love their enemies, did he mean that they should never kill them?

These are the central questions of this book.

Vicious bullies and ruthless dictators—Hitler, Stalin, Pol Pot, ISIS—swagger through history. They wreak terrible havoc on hundreds of millions of innocent people. In response, thoughtful, caring Christians and others regularly conclude that the only realistic way to stop their vile destruction is to kill them. In the face of such massive evil, pacifists—who claim that the followers of Jesus should love their enemies and never kill them—seem naive, simplistic, irresponsible.

Even worse, pacifists may appear to be fundamentally immoral. They seem to ignore their basic moral responsibility to love and therefore protect their neighbors. Standing passively on the sidelines and doing nothing to defend neighbors who are being destroyed is irresponsible and wicked.

C. S. Lewis makes the point vividly: "Does anyone suppose that our Lord's hearers understood him to mean that if a homicidal maniac, attempting to murder a third party, tried to knock me out of the way, I must stand aside and let him get his victim?"[1] Just war Christians regularly charge that pacifists fail to love their neighbors who are threatened. Pacifists, they allege, take no responsibility for history. They actually prefer tyranny to justice.

Both in my head and in my heart, I understand and appreciate the just war tradition. I think just war Christians are correct that if there are only two options (to kill or do nothing to defend neighbors), then faithful Christians should kill. C. S. Lewis is surely right. Jesus would not want us to step aside and passively watch while an aggressor brutalizes others.

The problem with this critique of pacifism is that there are never only two options: option one, to kill; option two, to do nothing. There is always a third possibility: intervening nonviolently to oppose and seek to restrain the aggressor. Nor is nonviolent resistance to evil a utopian, ineffective approach. In the past one hundred years (and especially the past fifty years), nonviolent resistance to injustice, tyranny, and brutal dictatorship has again and again proved astonishingly successful. Gandhi's nonviolence defeated the British Empire. Dr. Martin Luther King Jr.'s nonviolent civil rights movement changed American history. Solidarity's nonviolent campaign defied and conquered the Polish communist dictatorship. A million nonviolent Filipino demonstrators prevailed against a vicious dictator, President Ferdinand Marcos.[2] In fact, a recent scholarly book discovered amazing results: "Nonviolent resistance campaigns were nearly twice as likely to achieve full or partial success as their violent counterparts."[3]

It is simply contrary to the facts of history to say that there are only two options in the face of tyranny and brutality: to kill or to do nothing. I agree that to stand aside and fail to resist evil is cowardly, irresponsible, immoral, and blatantly contradictory to Jesus' command to love our neighbors. But the historical record demonstrates that there is always a third option: vigorous, nonviolent resistance. And it frequently works. Apparently it succeeds more often than violence.

But not always. Sometimes, at least in the short run, nonviolent actions fail. What then should Christians do?

Later I will examine the many arguments claiming that Christians today should not be bound by Jesus' teaching. But if Jesus is true God as well as true man; if the eternal Son became human not only to die for our sins but also to reveal how we should live; if Jesus claimed to be the long-expected Messiah; if central to Jesus' gospel is the announcement that the messianic kingdom is now breaking into history in the new community of Jesus' disciples, where forgiveness, justice, and peace reign; and if, in the power of the risen Lord, it is possible for Jesus' disciples to live *now* the norms of Jesus' dawning kingdom—if that is what the New Testament teaches (and this book will seek to show in detail that it is), then it is a huge theological mistake to say that contemporary Christians should ignore or set aside what Jesus taught about killing.

For the Christian who embraces historical orthodox teaching about who Jesus is, the most important question for our topic is this: Did Jesus mean to teach his disciples never to kill? This book is my answer.

As a careful reader, you have already noticed that I sometimes use the word *pacifism* to describe my position. I use that word to describe the view that it is always wrong to kill people.

Unfortunately, many people confuse the term *pacifism* with *passivism*. I totally reject a passivist approach, which stands aside and does nothing to resist evil, injustice, and oppression. Whenever I use pacifism in a positive way, I refer to an activist approach that vigorously challenges evil persons but refuses to kill them. Nonviolent action is central to the biblical pacifism advocated here.

QUESTIONS FOR REFLECTION AND DISCUSSION

1. What do most of your friends think of pacifists?

2. What are your strongest feelings about pacifists?

3. The author says that Jesus' teaching on the topic should be the most important factor in what Christians think and do on this topic. Do you agree or not? Why?

2

The Setting for Jesus' Radical Teaching

MOST CHRISTIANS KNOW that Jesus told his disciples to love their enemies. But they disagree on what he meant. Was Jesus talking only about personal enemies in one's immediate village? National enemies of one's country? All enemies? We cannot understand Jesus' command to love our enemies unless we have a clear picture of the setting in which Jesus spoke these amazing words. Understanding that setting is the task of this chapter.

Many Jews of Jesus' day were eagerly expecting a military messiah. This messianic warrior would drive out the oppressive Roman imperialists who ruled Palestine and establish a kingdom where God's will would prevail. Jesus claimed to be the expected messiah. But Jesus offered a radically different understanding of the messiah. As Messiah, he taught that his followers should love their enemies. And he said that dying on the cross was a central part of how he intended to establish the messianic kingdom.

To understand Jesus, we need to explore three things more deeply: first, the messianic expectations in Jesus' day; second, the extent of messianic violence in Jesus' time; and third, the meaning of Jesus' definition of the gospel as the "good news of the kingdom." Only then will we be ready to understand Jesus' more specific words and actions about violence.

MESSIANIC EXPECTATIONS IN JESUS' DAY

In 587 BC, Babylonians captured and destroyed Jerusalem, taking many Jews into exile. The prophets interpreted this terrible catastrophe as God's punishment for the nation's sins, especially idolatry and injustice. But the prophets also predicted a new day when the exiles would return to Jerusalem and God would be present in a rebuilt temple.

By the time of Jesus' birth, there was a widespread, intense expectation that a descendant of King David would come as a conquering military messiah to destroy Israel's enemies. One text put it bluntly:

> How beautiful is the king, the messiah, who will arise from those who are of the house of Judah! He girds up his loins and goes forth and orders the battle array against his enemies and slays the kings along with their overlords, and no king or overlord can stand before him; he reddens the mountains with the blood of their slain, his clothing is dipped in blood like a winepress.[1]

The New Testament scholar Craig Keener says, "Most Jews expected a final war against the Gentiles to culminate this age and inaugurate their redemption."[2]

In this time, many Jews understood three key passages in Isaiah about a future time of peace to refer to the expected messianic time (Isaiah 2:2-4; 9:5-7; 11:1-9). "They will beat their swords into plowshares and their spears into pruning hooks. Nation will not take up sword against nation" (Isaiah 2:4). But the time of universal peace would come only after the military messiah had conquered the Gentiles.

MESSIANIC VIOLENCE IN JESUS' TIME

Josephus, a first-century Jewish historian, is our best source (outside the New Testament) for life in Palestine at this time. At great length he describes how numerous religiously motivated (often messianic) movements urged the Jews to rebel against their Roman rulers. The result was the Jewish War (AD 66–70) in which the Romans totally destroyed Jerusalem.

The Jews had reason to resent their Roman conquerors. After Pompey's Roman soldiers conquered Palestine in 63 BC, Pompey walked right into the holy of holies in the temple in Jerusalem, which only the high priest was allowed to enter once a year. Roman taxation was heavy, and the threats to cherished Jewish religious beliefs were frequent. It is not surprising that a whole series of Jewish rebels rose up, urging the Jews to revolt against Rome. Sometimes they promised that God would intervene and send the messiah to establish the messianic kingdom if the people joined the battle against the Romans.

Herod the Great ruled Palestine as a client king of Rome from about 37 to 4 BC. He infuriated many Jews by imposing heavy taxes and building Roman temples honoring Caesar as divine. When he died, rebellion broke out.

Motivated partly by religious zeal, the rebels killed large numbers of Roman soldiers in Jerusalem. Josephus tells us that guerilla warfare was everywhere in Judea. But the Roman general in charge of Syria eventually arrived with a large contingent of Roman troops and squelched the rebellion, crucifying two thousand Jewish rebels.

In Galilee, in the city of Sepphoris (not far from Nazareth), Jewish rebels broke into Herod's arsenal and armed themselves. But Roman troops soon arrived, burned the city, and sold the inhabitants into slavery.

Ten years later another Jewish rebellion against Rome broke out when the Roman governor declared a census and taxation. The leaders urged the Jews to refuse to pay the tax and rebel. They promised the people that God would intervene if they joined the rebellion—quite possibly a promise with messianic implications. Josephus tells us that the leaders of this rebellion were the founders of a fourth Jewish philosophy (alongside the Pharisees, Sadducees, and Essenes). And Josephus explicitly says that it was this fourth philosophy (with its religious, perhaps messianic rejection of Roman rule and taxation) that eventually led to the devastating Jewish War in AD 66–70, which destroyed the nation.

Josephus tells us about many other Jewish outbreaks of rebellion against Rome in the period from AD 26 to 48. The evidence is clear. From the time of Herod I's death in 4 BC, there were repeated violent rebellions against Roman rule in Palestine. Both in Galilee and especially in Jerusalem, "revolution of one sort or another was in the air, and often present on the ground."[3] The sources often indicate a religious motivation. Frequently, as the New Testament scholar N. T. Wright points out, these movements "were led by messianic or quasi-messianic figures."[4] And the Romans frequently squelched them with crucifixion. Violent messianic revolt was grounded in the belief that God would intervene to bring the messianic kingdom if the Jews would dare to rebel; this was clearly part of Jewish life in this period.

JESUS' GOSPEL OF THE KINGDOM

Virtually every New Testament scholar today of every theological orientation agrees that the gospel Jesus announced was the good news of "the kingdom of God." The phrase appears 122 times in the first three gospels.

At the beginning of his gospel, Mark summarizes Jesus' whole message with the simple words: "The kingdom of God has come near. Repent and believe the good news" (Mark 1:15). Luke begins Jesus' public ministry with Jesus in the synagogue, reading Isaiah 61:1-2, a text often understood in that time as a passage about the coming messianic kingdom. Jesus ends the reading with the words, "Today this scripture is fulfilled in your hearing" (Luke 4:21). When opponents claim that Jesus is casting out demons by the power of Satan, he replies: "If it is by the Spirit of God that I drive out demons, then the kingdom of God has come upon you" (Matthew 12:28). The verb is in the present perfect tense, which means that the kingdom has already begun—and continues. The long-expected kingdom of God has already arrived. And it is happening through the work of Jesus himself—a clear, if indirect, claim to be the expected Messiah.

Jesus' declaration that the kingdom of God was arriving would have sparked enormous excitement among Jesus' contemporaries. As N. T. Wright says, "God's kingdom, to the Jew-in-the-village in the first half of the first century, meant the coming vindication of Israel, victory over the pagans, the eventual gift of peace, justice, and prosperity."[5]

But Jesus fundamentally reinterpreted his people's hope for the messianic kingdom. Nowhere is this clearer than in Jesus' rejection of the violent revolutionaries' call to take up arms against the Romans. These revolutionaries who opposed paying Roman taxes certainly denounced the Roman law that made it legal for a Roman soldier to demand that a person in a conquered territory carry his bags for one mile. Instead of urging rebellion against that law, Jesus called his followers to carry the bags a second mile (Matthew 5:41)! Instead of urging slaughter of the godless conquerors, Jesus urged his people to love their enemies.

Jesus' triumphal entry into Jerusalem the week before Passover provides one of the most powerful demonstrations of his understanding of a peaceful messiah (Matthew 21:1-11). That action was also one of Jesus' most explicit public claims to be the Messiah. Up to that time, Jesus had not encouraged public recognition of him as Messiah. Now he chooses to take a vivid public action that people would clearly understand to be a claim to be the expected messiah. He encourages crowds to accompany him into Jerusalem as if he were Davidic royalty. And he does it the week before Passover, when many Jews expected the messiah to appear.

But the way Jesus makes this public messianic claim vividly demonstrates that he rejects the popular expectation of the messiah as a conquering military hero. Jesus rides into Jerusalem on a humble donkey, not a military warhorse. He consciously chooses to appeal to the peaceful understanding of the messiah portrayed in the prophet Zechariah: "Lo, your king comes to you, . . . humble and riding on a donkey. . . . He will cut off the chariot from Ephraim and the war-horse from Jerusalem, . . . and he shall command peace to the nations" (Zechariah 9:9-10 NRSV). Jesus' action clearly says: I am the Messiah, but God's Messiah is not the conquering military messiah of popular expectation.

Many Jews in Jesus' day thought the messiah would come to inaugurate the kingdom if large numbers of people would join the rebels in a huge war against the Romans. Jesus rejected this violent messianic option, calling his disciples to love their enemies. As N. T. Wright explains, Jesus taught that the kingdom would come "not by military victory, but by a doubly revolutionary method: turning the other cheek, going the second mile, the deeply subversive wisdom of taking up the cross."[6]

Jesus' teaching on forgiveness also contrasted sharply with other messianic strategies. Some Pharisees taught that if the people kept the law faithfully, that would hasten the coming of the messiah. Jesus, on the other hand, taught that forgiveness was central to the arrival of the kingdom. The kingdom, Jesus said, is like a merciful king who freely forgives a huge debt that his servant cannot repay (Matthew 18:23-35). To the horror of the Pharisees, Jesus eagerly forgave even the most notorious offenders: prostitutes, the woman caught in adultery, and hated tax collectors profiting from collaboration with the foreign oppressors. Jesus forgave sinners in this radical, prodigal way because he knew that God is like the forgiving father in the parable of the prodigal son.

Jesus not only taught about a forgiving God; he also claimed personal authority to forgive sins. Jewish sources do not speak of the messiah forgiving sins on his own authority. But Jesus boldly claimed that authority. Jesus forgave the sins of the paralytic seeking healing. When the religious leaders objected to this blasphemous infringement on God's sole authority to forgive sins, he retorted: "I want you to know that the Son of Man has authority on earth to forgive sins" (Mark 2:10).

Jesus' teaching in general and the Sermon on the Mount in particular spell out how Jesus intended his new messianic community to live. The New Testament scholar Richard Hays points out that Matthew understands the Sermon on the Mount not as some impossible ideal but rather as "Jesus' programmatic disclosure of the kingdom of God and of the life to which the community of disciples is called."[7] And Jesus certainly was not thinking of his disciples as a tiny, isolated fringe group in Israel. He said his people should be the salt of the *earth* and the light of the *whole world* (Matthew 5:13-14). By appointing twelve disciples, he showed that his message was for the twelve tribes of Israel, for the whole nation.

And that message involved a radical challenge to the status quo at many points. He upset men who were happy with the easy divorce laws that enabled them to dismiss their wives for many reasons. Instead he insisted that God intended one man and one woman to live together in lifelong, joyful union. Jesus also disregarded social patterns that treated women as inferior.[8] Jesus upset political rulers, smugly satisfied with their domination of their subjects. In the dawning messianic age, servanthood must replace domination. Jesus terrified the economic establishment of his day. It would be easier for a camel to squeeze through the eye of a needle, he insisted, than for a rich person to enter the kingdom (Matthew 19:24).

In a daring act that led to his arrest, Jesus attacked the economic oppression and the religious desecration going on in the temple. Many people see only the religious side of Jesus' cleansing of the temple. But the text explicitly says that Jesus objected to both the sacrilege and the robbery: "It is written, 'My house shall be a house of prayer'; but you have made it a den of robbers" (Luke 19:46 NRSV). The chief priests and their collaborators with Rome had a monopoly on the sale of sacrificial animals, which Jewish worshipers who came from any distance had to purchase in order to sacrifice. Apparently they turned the temple's court of the Gentiles into a profitable stockyard, where they charged very high prices. Jesus denounces their des-ecration of the Gentiles' place of prayer for the sake of eco-nomic oppression.

It is hardly surprising that the authorities moved quickly to dispose of him (Luke 19:47). A person demanding such radical change from the rich and powerful was a dangerous revolution-ary. Jesus' uncompromising attack on the status quo where it was wrong was one fundamental reason he was crucified.

But Jesus' radical challenge to the status quo is only one part of the explanation for Jesus' death. The title Pilate placed on Jesus' cross, "King of the Jews," shows that the Romans cruci-fied him on the political charge of treason as a messianic pre-tender. And the Jewish leaders of the Sanhedrin charged him with blasphemy for acknowledging that he was "the Son of the Blessed One" and asserting that they would see him "sitting at the right hand of the Mighty One" (Mark 14:61-64).

Jesus, however, went to the cross not just because others hated what he said and did. The Gospels also tell us that Jesus thought his death was central to his mission. The Son of Man (his favorite title for himself) came, Jesus said, "to give his life as a ransom for many" (Matthew 20:28). Both Matthew and Mark report that immediately after Jesus affirmed Peter's confession that he was the Messiah, Jesus began to warn the disciples about his coming death (Matthew 16:13-23; Mark 8:27-33). At the last meal with his disciples, Jesus said his blood "is poured out for many for the forgiveness of sins" (Matthew 26:28).

N. T. Wright shows that Jesus' view of his death was central to his belief that the kingdom of God was actually arriving in his own person. Jesus' contemporaries expected the messiah to cleanse or rebuild the temple and defeat their enemies. Jesus seems to suggest that his death would accomplish what Jews generally thought the temple accomplished (he had already claimed authority to forgive sins apart from the temple). "In other words," Wright says, "Jesus intended that his death should in some sense function sacrificially."[9] His death would also conquer the real enemy, who was not the Romans but Satan, "who had duped YHWH's [Yahweh's] people into themselves taking the pagan route, seeking to bring YHWH's kingdom by force of arms and military revolt."[10]

The cross, then, is also central to Jesus' understanding of the kingdom of God—as is the resurrection. If Jesus had remained dead, the only conceivable conclusion for a Jew would have been that he was a failed, false messiah.

Too often in the history of Christianity, Christians have focused exclusively (or largely) on only the life and teaching of Christ or only the death of Christ. Even the Apostles' Creed and the Nicene Creed move directly from Jesus' birth to his death, as if nothing important happened in between. That is to belittle or ignore Jesus' teaching and undermine discipleship and ethical obedience. The widespread and heretical idea in many evangelical circles—that the only important reason Jesus came was to die for our sins—is one of the most glaring examples of failure to embrace the full biblical Christ. Tragically, other Christians seem to affirm the equally heretical idea that it is only Jesus' teaching—especially his call to love enemies— that is finally important. If we believe that the teacher from Nazareth is God incarnate, as the church through two millennia has believed, then we must embrace the full biblical Christ. We will examine the crucifixion more in chapter 12.

Jesus' gospel of the kingdom of God includes his announcement of the kingdom, his teaching about the kingdom, and his actual inauguration of the kingdom in his life, death, and resurrection. Lisa Sharon Harper is right: "The good news was both about the *coming* of the Kingdom of God and the *character* of that Kingdom. It was about what God's Kingdom looked like."[11] The gospel provides the context for us to explore in detail, in the next two chapters, what his teachings tell us about our basic question: Does Jesus ever want his disciples to kill?

QUESTIONS FOR REFLECTION AND DISCUSSION

1. What kind of messiah did Jews in Jesus' day expect?

2. What historical evidence is there that around the time of Jesus, many rebellions against Rome broke out among devout Jews? And why is it important to see that these rebels were devoutly religious Jews, often with intense messianic hopes?

3. Why did the Jews resent the Romans?

4. Do the Christians you know define the gospel the way Jesus did? If not, what is the difference?

5. How does Jesus' messianic understanding differ from the widespread Jewish expectation?

6. What are several reasons for Jesus' death? Do most Christians emphasize all these reasons?

7. How does one's understanding of Jesus change if one embraces only one of the reasons for Jesus' death?

3

Living in Jesus' Dawning Kingdom

WE CAN ONLY understand Jesus' teaching in the context of his gospel of the kingdom. Jesus taught that the long-expected messianic kingdom was actually breaking into history in a powerful way in his actions and disciples. And Jesus' teaching explained how Jesus expected his followers to live in that new kingdom.

It is clear that Jesus intended his ethical teaching to be for everyone, not only some little group. At the end of the Sermon on the Mount, Jesus insists that "everyone who hears these words of mine and puts them into practice is like the wise man who built his house on the rock" (Matthew 7:24). At the end of his gospel, Matthew reports that Jesus sent his disciples into the whole world not only to baptize those who believe but to teach them "everything I have commanded you" (28:20). Jesus wants his followers to be "the salt of the earth" and "the light of the world" (5:13-14). Jesus' kingdom ethics, which his disciples now live, is the way God wants everyone to live.

The Sermon on the Mount in Matthew 5–7 is the largest block of Jesus' teaching in all four Gospels. So we must start there to look for an answer to our question, Does Jesus ever want his disciples to kill their enemies?

TWO VIEWS ON THE SERMON ON THE MOUNT

Matthew 5:21-48 contains a set of sayings where Jesus says something like this: "You have heard that it was said, . . . but I say to you." In at least some cases, Jesus seems to refer to an Old Testament teaching that he then sets aside. But immediately before this block of material, Jesus insists that he came not to abolish the Law and the Prophets "but to fulfill them." Jesus even adds that "until heaven and earth disappear, not the smallest letter . . . will by any means disappear from the Law until everything is accomplished" (Matthew 5:17-18).

What does Jesus mean?

Throughout church history and still today, there are two quite different answers to that question. Some argue that Jesus did not set aside any Old Testament law or teaching. He merely corrected misunderstandings of the Old Testament held by some of his contemporaries. Others believe that Jesus fulfilled some parts of the Old Testament precisely by setting aside some of its provisions and calling his disciples to a different, higher norm. We must examine Jesus' explicit words in Matthew 5:21-48 to see which view fits better with what Jesus actually says.

It is important, however, to remember that Jesus and the early church did set aside some significant Old Testament teachings. Keeping Old Testament food laws, which commanded Jews not to eat certain foods, was an important part of first-century Jewish life. But "Jesus declared all foods clean" (Mark 7:18-19). Strict observance of the Sabbath was one of the most important parts of Jewish life in Jesus' day. But Jesus defended his disciples when the Pharisees charged his disciples with breaking Sabbath laws. Jesus even dares to claim authority over the Sabbath. "The Sabbath was made for people, not people for the Sabbath. So the Son of Man is Lord even of the Sabbath" (Mark 2:27-28 TNIV).

But we must carefully examine the antitheses ("You have heard that it was said, . . . but I say to you") in Matthew 5:21-48 to explore carefully the question, Does Jesus' teaching never set aside Old Testament teaching, or does Jesus sometimes fulfill the Old Testament by teaching that his kingdom ethic sometimes goes beyond and is different from the Old Testament?

It appears that Jesus claimed the authority to challenge widely understood demands of the law. And the early Christians clearly taught that central demands of the Old Testament law— circumcision, food laws, sacrifices in the temple for forgiveness of sins, the Sabbath—were no longer binding. Paul taught that although the law was a divinely given custodian applicable until the coming of Christ, now "we are no longer under a guardian" (Galatians 3:25). As the New Testament scholar R. T. France notes, if Matthew 5:17-20 means that the rules of the Old Testament law must be followed "as they were before Jesus came," Matthew would "here be contradicting the whole tenor of the NT by declaring that, for instance, the sacrificial and food laws of the OT are still binding on Jesus' disciples."[1]

SIX ANTITHESES

We must carefully examine each of Jesus' six antitheses. Does Jesus simply correct misunderstandings of Old Testament texts, or does he sometimes fulfill them by transcending them? And what does that tell us about the basic questions of this book?

MURDER AND ADULTERY

The first two sets of sayings, on murder (Matthew 5:21-26) and adultery (5:27-30), clearly show Jesus strengthening but certainly not setting aside Old Testament commands. Not only should Jesus' followers not murder; they also should not even be angry with a sister or brother. Not only should they not commit adultery; they also should avoid dwelling on lustful thoughts.

DIVORCE

The segment on divorce appears somewhat different. In Matthew 5:31, Jesus quotes Deuteronomy 24:1, where the Mosaic law forbids a husband who has divorced a wife (who then marries another man) from taking her back later. The Deuteronomic text does not command divorce, but it clearly allows it. Later, in Matthew 19:3-9, the Pharisees ask Jesus, "Why . . . did Moses command that a man give his wife a certificate of divorce?" (v. 7). Jesus replies that Moses permitted divorce "because your hearts were hard," but that was never God's will. And Jesus insists that his disciples follow the Creator's original intention, rejecting divorce "except for sexual immorality" (v. 9).

This teaching of Jesus does not set aside an explicit Old Testament command. But it does set aside what the Mosaic law allowed. In fact, in his widely used book *Jerusalem in the Time of Jesus*, German scholar Joachim Jeremias says Jesus "unhesitatingly and fearlessly criticized the Torah for permitting divorce."[2]

OATHS

In Matthew 5:33-37, Jesus condemns all use of oaths: "Again, you have heard that it was said to the people long ago, 'Do not break your oath,' . . . But I tell you, do not swear . . . at all. . . .

All you need to say is simply 'Yes' or 'No'; anything beyond this comes from the evil one."

The Old Testament not only forbids breaking one's oath (see Leviticus 19:12); it also explicitly *commands* taking oaths. In Numbers 5:19-22, the text directs the priest to have a woman take an oath. Deuteronomy 6:13 declares: "Fear the Lord your God, serve him only and take your oaths in his name." Exodus 22:10-11 explicitly prescribes that a dispute "will be settled by the taking of an oath before the Lord."

Here in Matthew 5:33-37, Jesus clearly forbids what the Old Testament commands. And James 5:12 shows that the early church remembered and sought to live by Jesus' prohibition of oaths: "Above all, my brothers and sisters, do not swear—not by heaven or by earth or by anything else. All you need to say is a simple 'Yes' or 'No.' Otherwise, you will be condemned."

EYE FOR AN EYE

Matthew 5:38-42 is a very important text for our question. Here it is, from Jesus Christ as reported by Matthew:

> You have heard that it was said, "Eye for eye, and tooth for tooth." But I tell you, do not resist an evil person. If anyone slaps you on the right check, turn to them the other cheek also. And if anyone wants to sue you and take your shirt, hand over your coat as well. If anyone forces you to go one mile, go with them two miles. Give to the one who asks you, and do not turn away from the one who wants to borrow from you.[3]

This eye-for-an-eye retaliation had been a central principle of Near Eastern law since the famous Code of Hammurabi (eighteenth century BC). And it was certainly the keynote of the Old Testament teaching on criminal justice. Exodus 21:23-24 is clear: "If there is serious injury, you are to take life for life, eye for eye, tooth for tooth." Leviticus states the same standard: "Anyone who injures [a] neighbor is to be injured in the same manner: fracture for fracture, eye for eye, tooth for tooth" (24:19-20; compare also Deuteronomy 19:19-21).

Jesus' response to this fundamental Old Testament principle is pointed: "But I tell you, do not resist an evil person" (Matthew 5:39). In a moment, we will carefully examine what the key verb translated in the NIV as "do not resist" actually means. But to try to argue, as some do, that here Jesus is not setting aside an Old Testament teaching seems to ignore the clear meaning of the text.

Central to an understanding of this passage is the proper translation of the key verb *antistēnai*. The NIV translates it "do not resist." And a number of people have concluded that Jesus advocates pure passivity, total nonresistance in the face of evil.

But if Jesus in Matthew 5:39 is advocating pure passivity in the face of evil, then Jesus again and again contradicts his own teaching. Jesus unleashes a blistering attack on the Pharisees, denouncing them as blind guides, fools, hypocrites, and snakes (Matthew 23:13-33). He urges his followers to confront members of the church who sin (18:15-17). His cleansing of the temple, when he overturns the tables of money changers and drives out the animals, is anything but passive (21:12-13). And at his trial, when an official slaps him on the cheek, he protests (John 18:22-23).

A careful study of the verb used in this text shows clearly that Jesus is not recommending passivity. The Greek term for "resist" used in Matthew 5:39 appears in the Greek Old Testament primarily as a military term. In forty-four of seventy-one uses in the Greek Old Testament, the word refers to armed resistance in military encounters (as in Leviticus 26:37; Deuteronomy 7:24; 25:18; Joshua 7:13; 23:9; Judges 2:14). Josephus, the first-century Jewish historian, uses the word fifteen of seventeen times to refer to violent struggle.

N. T. Wright summarizes the meaning of the term this way: "The word 'resist' is *antistēnai*, almost a technical term for revolutionary resistance of a specifically military variety. Taken in this sense, the command draws out the implication of a good deal of the sermon so far. The way forward for Israel is not the way of violent resistance . . . but the different, oblique way of creative non-violent resistance. . . . Jesus' people were not to become part of the resistance movement."[4]

After prohibiting a violent response to evil, the text describes a proper response in four concrete situations. In each case, the commanded response is neither violent nor passive. Jesus calls his disciples not to turn aside passively or hit back, but rather to confront the evil nonviolently. Jesus seems to urge a vigorously activist (although certainly nonviolent) response to evil and injustice.[5]

Turn the other cheek

The text says: "If anyone slaps you on the right cheek, turn to them the other cheek also" (Matthew 5:39). In the usual positions, a right-handed person could strike another individual on the right cheek only with the back of the hand. We know from documents of the time that a backhand blow to the right cheek was a huge insult. A backhand slap was reserved for "inferiors" like slaves and wives.

Jesus' advice to turn the other cheek—the left one—seems to convey a surprising suggestion. Normally an inferior would simply accept the insult (or on occasion fight back). But by turning the *left* cheek to the person delivering the insult, one almost forces the attacker to use his fist if he wants to strike again. (It is much harder to hit the left cheek with a backslap than with a fist.) The effect is that the person of lower status astonishes his superior by a dramatic act that asserts his dignity, but not by striking back. Instead, the person forces his attacker either to stop hitting him *or* to use his fist and thus treat him as an equal. Thus Jesus urges a nonviolent but nonetheless activist response to evil.

Sued for one's coat

"If anyone wants to sue you and take your shirt [inner garment], hand over your coat [outer garment] as well" (Matthew 5:40).[6] The setting refers to a typical first-century context in which debt was widespread among the poor. Jesus tells many parables about people in debt.

In Jesus' example, the person taken to court for an unpaid debt is obviously very poor; he apparently owns nothing of worth to repay the debt except his clothes. As an impoverished person, he has no hope of winning a court case against the richer person. So he loses his inner garment as payment on his debt. But why would Jesus tell this kind of poor person, who has just lost his inner garment, to also give the person to whom he owes money his outer garment as well? Since many poor people had only one outer garment, that would mean stripping naked in court! And nakedness was a terrible disgrace in Palestinian Jewish society.

The disgrace for nakedness fell not only on the naked person but also on those viewing the naked person (Genesis 9:20-27).

By stripping naked, the debtor exposes the cruelty not only of the creditor but also of the oppressive system he represents. Rather than recommending a passive response to injustice, Jesus again urges a dramatic nonviolent protest.

The second mile

"If anyone forces you to go one mile, go with them two miles" (Matthew 5:41). The context for this saying clearly is Roman imperialism. The word translated "mile" is a Roman word, not a Jewish word. And the word translated "forces you" is the technical term (verb, *angareuō*; noun, *angareia*) widely known in Roman law to refer to the legal right of Roman soldiers to compel subject people to carry their packs for one mile. Roman soldiers often abused this right, and colonized people hated this burdensome obligation.

In chapter 2 we saw how angry, violent rebellion against Roman rule and its collaborators kept erupting among the Jews in the century around the time of Jesus. These violent revolutionaries certainly urged fellow Jews to refuse to carry the baggage of oppressive Roman soldiers. Jesus recommends the precise opposite! The words used and the context demonstrate that Jesus is clearly rejecting a widespread, popular attitude toward the oppressive Roman imperialists.

But is he recommending passivity? The soldier knows the colonized person has a legal obligation to carry his pack one mile. But he also knows the law forbids the Roman soldier to force the person to carry it more than one mile. And he knows his commander may punish him severely for breaking this law. So when they reach the end of the first mile, the soldier asks for the return of his pack. But the person offers to carry it another mile. Now the soldier is in trouble. He may be disciplined by his superior. So he begs to be given back his pack. "Imagine the situation of a Roman infantryman pleading with a Jew to give back his pack!" writes biblical scholar Walter Wink. "The humor of this scene may have escaped us, but it would scarcely have been lost on Jesus' hearers, who must have been regaled at the prospect of thus discomfiting their oppressors."[7]

With this action, the oppressed Jew seizes the initiative and asserts his dignity—but all in a nonviolent way, fully compatible with loving the oppressor without endorsing the oppression.

"LOVE YOUR ENEMIES"

It is hard to exaggerate either the originality or the importance of Jesus' direct command to love our enemies. Let's look at his words.

> You have heard that it was said, "Love your neighbor and hate your enemy." But I tell you, love your enemies and pray for those who persecute you, that you may be children of your Father in heaven. He causes his sun to rise on the evil and the good, and sends rain on the righteous and the unrighteous. If you love those who love you, what reward will you get? Are not even the tax collectors doing that? And if you greet only your own people, what are you doing more than others? Do not even pagans do that? Be perfect, therefore, as your heavenly Father is perfect. (Matthew 5:43-48)

The summons to "love your neighbor" is a direct quote from the Greek translation of Leviticus 19:18.

But who are those who call people to "hate your enemy"? Who does Jesus have in mind? We know that the manual of discipline of Jesus' contemporaries, the Essenes (known to us from the Dead Sea Scrolls), explicitly says, "Love all the sons of light, . . . and . . . hate all the sons of darkness." In Jesus' day, some of the Jewish revolutionaries certainly agreed. Who are the enemies Jesus summons his disciples to love? It is interesting that in Matthew 5:43 ("Love your neighbor and hate your enemy"), the words for "neighbor" and "enemy" are singular. But verse 44 uses the plural: "Love your enemies." Every class of enemy seems to be included.

New Testament scholar Richard Hays points out that the term *echthroi* (enemies) is generic. It "is often used in biblical Greek of national or military enemies."[8] For example, in Deuteronomy 20:1, the text says: "When you go to war against your enemies [*echthroi*] and see horses and chariots and an army greater than yours, do not be afraid of them." This verse follows immediately after Deuteronomy 19:21, which commands an eye for an eye—the principle that Jesus specifically rejects. After a major review of recent scholarly literature on the topic, the German scholar Heinz-Wolfgang Kuhn concludes that the enemies Jesus calls his disciples to love include everyone. "The directive is without boundaries. The religious, the political, and the personal are all meant. Every enemy is meant."[9]

Martin Hengel, one of the leading scholars on the nationalist, revolutionary Jewish movements of Jesus' time, thinks that Jesus' command to love one's enemies "was formulated with direct reference to the theocratic and nationalistic liberation movement in which hatred toward an enemy was regarded as a good work."[10] There is no way to prove that decisively. But in the immediately preceding section, Jesus has urged his followers to carry the packs of Roman soldiers not just the legally mandated one mile but also a second mile. Thus Jesus is thinking about the situation that the violent Jewish revolutionaries hated. If in verse 41 Jesus is talking about how to respond to

Roman imperialists, it is very likely that his command to love enemies includes the people whom the revolutionaries sought to kill.

Jesus' stated reason for loving one's enemies is important. His disciples should act that way so "that you may be children of your Father in heaven" (v. 45). The same teaching about loving enemies appears in the gospel of Luke. There too, as in Matthew, it is a major part of Jesus' first ethical teaching.

Jesus' command to love our enemies contradicts the practice of every society known to historians. No precise parallel to Jesus' words has been found. New Testament scholars point out that the saying appears both in the "earliest sayings" tradition of Jesus' words (scholars call this source "Q") and then in Luke (6:27, 35) as well as in Matthew. The evidence leads Martin Hengel to say that "this Magna Charta of *agape* [love]" is what is "actually revolutionary in the message of Jesus."[11] There is no other ethical issue about which the New Testament says Jesus' disciples are like the heavenly Father when they act a certain way.

Also striking is the fact that Matthew 5:38-48 is probably the most frequently cited biblical text when one collects all the statements about killing from the early Christian writers before the time of Constantine. Ten different writers in at least twenty-eight different places cite or refer to this passage and note that Christians love their enemies and turn the other cheek. In nine instances, they link this passage from Jesus with a statement that Christians are peaceable, ignorant of war, or opposed to attacking others. Sometimes they explicitly link Jesus' saying to a rejection of killing and war.[12] In every single instance in which pre-Constantinian Christian writers mention the topic of killing, they say that Christians do not do that, whether in abortion, capital punishment, or war. And Jesus' statement about loving enemies is one of the reasons cited.

QUESTIONS FOR REFLECTION AND DISCUSSION

1. Do you think that Jesus' ethical teaching is for everyone? Did Jesus? What difference does it make?

2. What are the two views on how Jesus fulfills the Old Testament?

3. Which of those positions do you think Jesus' antitheses in Matthew 5:21-48 seem to support? Where, if anywhere, does Jesus set aside the Old Testament? How is your answer to this question important?

4. Why is Jesus' statement about "an eye for an eye" so important?

5. What does the verb translated "do not resist" mean? How might this change your and other people's understanding of this passage?

6. If Jesus is not proposing a passive nonresistance, how can we live out Jesus' call?

7. Who are the enemies Jesus calls us to love? Who are they in your life?

4

Further Claims of Jesus and How Christians Evade Them

THE SERMON ON the Mount appears to reject killing, as we've seen. Jesus' statements in several other places in Scripture seem to point in the same direction. We must explore these passages carefully. Later, then, we can look at the reasons many Christians believe Jesus did not mean to tell us never to kill.

OTHER TEACHINGS

Luke 4:16-20 depicts Jesus in the synagogue in his hometown reading from Isaiah 61:1-2. Some Jews in Jesus' day understood this text to be speaking of the messianic time. What is striking is that Jesus seems to end his reading in the middle of Isaiah 61:2. He omits the words "the day of vengeance of our God." Did Jesus omit those words to reject Jewish expectations of vengeance on their enemies? And did he instead want to speak of an expansion of God's covenant to include all people?

The following verses lend weight to that interpretation. In Luke 4, Jesus goes on to talk about two prominent Old Testament prophets ministering to and healing people who were Israel's national enemies. Jesus says Elijah was sent to a Baal-worshiping widow in the pagan city of Sidon (Luke 4:26; compare 1 Kings 17:8-24). And Elisha healed Naaman the Syrian (Luke 4:27). Naaman was not just a pagan. He was also the commander of the Syrian army, which had recently defeated Israel (2 Kings 5:1-19). Naaman was a national enemy! Jesus' two references point out the fact that prominent Old Testament prophets acted in love toward their national enemies. The implication seems to be that Jesus' messianic kingdom welcomes and loves even national enemies.

Not surprisingly, the devout Jews of Nazareth were furious. They tried to throw Jesus off a high cliff at the edge of town (Luke 4:28-29).

JESUS AND THE SAMARITANS

Jesus' attitude toward the Samaritans provides a striking example of loving one's enemies. In Jesus' time, Jews and Samaritans hated each other. Conflict, even bloody encounters, often occurred when Jewish pilgrims from Galilee traveled through Samaria on their way to Jerusalem for festivals. We see this bitter hostility exemplified in the Gospels when Jesus is refused lodging because he is on his way to Jerusalem (Luke 9:52-53) and is even refused a drink by the Samaritan woman (John 4:9). Jews and Samaritans were enemies!

Seen in this context, Jesus' dealings with Samaritans provide an astonishing example of loving national enemies. He praises the faith of a Samaritan (Luke 17:16, 18-19). He rejects his disciples' desire to call down fire from heaven on Samaritans who insult him (Luke 9:51-56). Jesus accepts a Samaritan woman as one of his earliest evangelists (John 4:1-42). He even makes a Samaritan the hero of one of his most famous parables.

Indeed, when Jesus made a hated Samaritan the hero of this powerful parable, he must have incensed many of his Jewish listeners. In the parable, two Jewish leaders (a priest and a Levite) ignore and fail to help a half-dead victim of robbers, lying naked by the roadside. But then a Samaritan traveler stops, gently cares for the wounded man, puts him on his donkey, transports him to the nearest inn, and pays the innkeeper to care for him. At the end of the story, Jesus forces the learned expert on the Jewish law to admit that it was really the hated Samaritan who had acted as a neighbor. Rubbing it in, Jesus tells him to imitate the Samaritan (Luke 10:25-37)!

Every Jewish listener to Jesus' words would have known without any question that Jesus was making a hero out of their nation's enemy. Love for one's enemy is a central implication of this parable. Indeed, all of Jesus' encounters with Samaritans seem to teach the same point.

HEALING A CENTURION'S SERVANT

Matthew 8:5-13 tells the story of a centurion who begs Jesus to heal his sick servant. As a military commander in charge of one hundred Roman soldiers, he represented the hated Roman imperialists, who controlled the land of the Jews. He was a visible symbol of the foreign conquerors the violent Jewish revolutionaries wanted to overthrow!

But Jesus offers to come to his house to heal his servant (v. 7). Jesus is amazed at his faith: "Truly I tell you, I have not found anyone in Israel with such great faith" (v. 10). But even more amazing is Jesus' next sentence: "I say to you that many will come from the east and the west, and will take their places at the feast with Abraham, Isaac and Jacob in the kingdom of heaven" (v. 11). Jesus tells the centurion that his dawning messianic kingdom is not just for Jews. It is for people from everywhere.

This story not only depicts Jesus associating with and healing the servant of the most visible symbol of the Jews' national enemy. It also clearly implies that Jesus' dawning kingdom welcomes those enemies as members.

DEALING WITH CONFLICT IN THE CHURCH

In Matthew 18, Jesus provides a process for dealing with sin in the church (vv. 15-20). First, go alone to the person sinning and seek restoration. If the first step fails, have two or three others join the conversation. If that fails, take it to the whole church.

There is nothing in this text that speaks about killing. But the text does present a nonviolent way to resolve conflict. To be a human community is to have conflict and sinful behavior. The typical response is to use violence to solve the problem. Jesus' teaching here offers a nonviolent procedural alternative.

"FATHER, FORGIVE THEM"

Luke tells us that after the soldiers had nailed Jesus to the cross, Jesus uttered the amazing words: "Father, forgive them, for they do not know what they are doing" (Luke 23:34). By any ordinary understanding, people spiking someone to a cross are enemies. But Jesus offers even these wicked people his love and forgiveness. Jesus' action and words on the cross are a powerful illustration of his teaching to love one's enemies.

JESUS AND THE SUFFERING SERVANT OF ISAIAH 40–55

Isaiah 40–55, and especially the servant song in Isaiah 52:13–53:12, were probably central in Jesus' understanding of his mission.

For Jews in Jesus' day, Isaiah 40–55 confirmed their expectation that God would soon end their exile, punish the pagans who held them captive, and return to Zion as king. And there is clear evidence that some Jews at this time understood the servant in Isaiah in a messianic way. But these Jewish thinkers definitely did not speak of a *suffering* messiah. They expected a conquering military hero.

Jesus agreed that the servant song of Isaiah 52:13–53:12 speaks of the messiah. But Jesus sees a messiah who suffers for others. Drawing on Isaiah's picture of the suffering servant, Jesus offers a peaceful messianic strategy, one that involves loving enemies even when that means being crucified.

"ALL WHO DRAW THE SWORD WILL DIE BY THE SWORD"

All four Gospels tell us that at Jesus' arrest someone (Peter, according to John 18:10-11) drew a sword and struck a person coming to arrest Jesus. And in each gospel, Jesus rebukes his would-be defender and commands him to stop using the sword.

Matthew gives a general reason for that command: "All who draw the sword will die by the sword" (Matthew 26:52). This general reason seems to imply a prohibition of all uses of the sword.

JESUS' DISCIPLES MUST "TAKE UP THEIR CROSS"

We have seen how Jesus' messianic understanding differed sharply from widespread views in his time. Many Jews expected a militaristic messiah who would lead the war against the Romans. And some taught that God would intervene to send the messiah and bring victory if the Jewish people would dare to take up the sword.

But Jesus' actions and his teaching show that Jesus rejected that violent path. Instead, he chose the cross. And repeatedly, Jesus also taught that his disciples must take up their own cross.

All three synoptic gospels—Matthew, Mark, and Luke—describe the same sequence of events. Peter confesses that Jesus is the Messiah. Jesus immediately predicts his rejection by the Jewish leaders and his death. Peter, still failing to understand Jesus' peaceful messianic understanding, takes Jesus aside and rebukes him for talking about rejection and death. In response, Jesus denounces Peter as Satan for his violent interpretation.

In all three synoptic gospels, Jesus' demand that his disciples also take up their cross follows immediately. Again and again, Jesus repeats this demand that his disciples take up their cross and follow him (Matthew 10:38; 16:24; Mark 8:34; Luke 9:23). Very clearly, each evangelist intends to teach that Jesus' disciples must follow Jesus in choosing the cross rather than violence.

SIDESTEPPING JESUS' TEACHING

Over the centuries, Christians have offered various reasons for thinking that Christians do not need to follow Jesus' call to love, rather than kill, their enemies.

JESUS CAME TO DIE

Many Christians think that the only important reason Jesus came was to die as the substitute for our sins. The gospel, they say, is only or primarily the good news that we are forgiven through the cross and can go to heaven when we die. Jesus' ethical teaching is at best relatively unimportant and perhaps irrelevant.

The problem with this understanding is that it simply ignores Jesus' full teaching about his gospel. As we saw in chapter 2, Jesus' gospel is the good news that the long-expected messianic kingdom is now breaking into history. Certainly one fundamental part of that good news is that God forgives sinners and that Jesus' death on the cross has accomplished our reconciliation with God. But equally central to Jesus' understanding of the gospel is the fact that the new messianic time of peace and justice has already begun and that Jesus' disciples are now summoned to live according to Jesus' teaching.

AN INTERIM ETHIC

Since the writing of Albert Schweitzer at the beginning of the twentieth century, many scholars have thought that Jesus expected an almost immediate end to our space-time world. Since the world was about to end, Jesus could proclaim a radical ethic for this brief interim—an ethic that would be totally unrealistic if the world were to continue.

The problem with this argument, as N. T. Wright clearly demonstrates, is that there is virtually no evidence that any Jew in Jesus' day thought that the arrival of the messianic kingdom meant the end of our space-time world.[1] The apocalyptic language used to describe the arrival of the messianic kingdom is figurative, underlining the sweeping societal change that the messiah would bring. Since Jesus was not thinking of a very near end of the world, the idea that his teaching offered an interim ethic for that short time makes no historical sense. It is a fiction of modern scholarship.

JESUS' RADICAL ETHIC CALLS US TO REPENTANCE, NOT DISCIPLESHIP

Believing that Jesus' radical ethics are impossible to live, some Christians (including Martin Luther) argue that the purpose of Jesus' ethics is to reveal our sinful failure and thus drive us to confess our sins and seek forgiveness rather than to actually reveal how Jesus wants his disciples to live.

Jesus' high demands rightly lead us to repentance. But there is not a hint in Jesus' teachings that he *only* calls for repentance. Throughout the Gospels, we see Jesus summoning his followers to obey his teaching. And as the risen Jesus leaves his disciples, he commands them to spread the gospel everywhere and teach the new disciples to "obey everything I have commanded you" (Matthew 28:19-20).

JESUS' ETHIC IS FOR SOME FUTURE ESCHATOLOGICAL KINGDOM, NOT THE PRESENT

Dispensational theology used to teach that since the Jews rejected Jesus as Messiah, the messianic kingdom was postponed until the millennium. Therefore Jesus' ethical teaching in the Sermon on the Mount and elsewhere does not apply today.

This view fails to understand Jesus' basic understanding of the gospel: the kingdom is now breaking in, and his disciples can and should live now according to his teaching. Furthermore, it is strange to say that a teaching like "Love your enemies" is not for the present (when Christians *do* have real enemies) but only for the millennium (when evil has been conquered and enemies no longer exist).

PRIVATE VERSUS PUBLIC ROLES

Various versions of this argument are probably the most common way Christians have argued that Jesus' command to love enemies does not mean that Christians should never kill others. Many Christians say that, as soldiers or public officials carrying out a judicial decision on capital punishment, Christians rightly kill. Jesus' teaching about how to respond to a slap of the hand or a demand for one's clothing shows, it is argued, that he is talking about how to respond to personal injury and not about public life. These Christians maintain that Jesus is talking about how one person responds to a single individual, not how one responds in a complex social setting when there are multiple neighbors under attack from evil persons.

Proponents of this view often argue that Romans 12:9-21 ("Do not repay anyone evil for evil"; leave vengeance to God) applies to the *personal* life of Christians in the church. They claim that Romans 13:1-7 (that government is "God's servant" to punish the evildoer) prescribes the *public* responsibilities, including serving in the army, that Christians have as citizens. Yes, one of the Ten Commandments prohibits killing; but these Christians argue the Old Testament clearly commands the death penalty and war. The proper conclusion, they say, is that as a private individual, one dare not kill, but as a person serving in a public role, one rightly kills. That, it is argued, is the assumption behind Romans 12–13.

Martin Luther's two-kingdom theology is one common version of this private-public distinction. Every Christian, Luther says, lives in two kingdoms. In the "kingdom of Christ" (seen most clearly in the church), the individual Christian loves enemies and does not resist evil. But in the "kingdom of the world," the same person occupies a public office (perhaps as judge or soldier) and rightly restrains evil, even with the sword.

Careful consideration of this widely used argument is essential. I believe this argument: 1) ignores the historical context of Jesus' teaching; 2) contradicts what seems to be the most obvious meaning of the text; 3) relies on pragmatism to set aside Jesus; 4) historically has sometimes led to very bad consequences; and 5) ignores the first three centuries of Christian teaching about killing.

In his historical context, Jesus claimed to be the Messiah of the entire Jewish people. Jews of all kinds—common people and religious leaders, ordinary folk and members of the Sanhedrin—heard his teaching. And it is clear that Jesus disagreed with the devout, violent Jewish revolutionaries of his time who, according to Josephus, urged the Jews to rebel against the Roman imperialists and their Jewish collaborators. Rejecting the widespread expectation of a military messiah, Jesus clearly chose to be a peaceful Messiah. Jesus called his followers to love even their enemies—and those enemies, as the saying about carrying Roman soldiers' packs a second mile demonstrates, included even the hated Romans.

As his response to several centuries of violent Jewish response to foreign oppressors, Jesus advocated love, even for political enemies. And there is certainly no hint that Jesus' reason for objecting to the violence of the revolutionaries was that they were unauthorized individuals whose violent swords would have been legitimate if the religiopolitical leaders of the Sanhedrin had just given the order. Rather, his point was that the revolutionaries' whole approach to enemies was wrong. They offered one messianic strategy; Jesus offered another. But both appealed to the entire Jewish nation to follow their vision and teaching. Jesus' call to love enemies clearly cannot be limited to the personal sphere of private life.

Second, the personal-public distinction seems to contradict the most natural, literal meaning of the text. The text gives no hint of such a distinction. It is true that one or two of Jesus' concrete examples refer to personal life. That is true of the slap on the cheek. To some extent, that is also the case with the statement about how the debtor should respond. But in that case, the setting is a court scene of public law. The call to carry the Roman soldier's pack a second mile clearly speaks of the public political setting where Roman imperialists had the legal right to make oppressive demands. And Jesus' call to reject the principle of "an eye for an eye" refers to the foundational principle of all Near Eastern jurisprudence. Jesus is talking about the very center of public life, not some personal private sphere. The Swiss New Testament scholar Eduard Schweizer is surely correct: "There is not the slightest hint of any realm where the disciple is not bound by the words of Jesus."[2] The most natural conclusion is that Jesus intended his words to be normative in both private and also public life.

Third, an essential ethical pragmatism often underlies the argument that Jesus could not have meant that his followers should never use lethal violence. Many argue that in our violent world, Jesus' love ethic simply will not work. This factual claim may or may not be accurate. But surely the *pragmatic* question of whether Jesus' ethic works in the short run—that is, whether it enables us and others to avoid suffering—dare not be decisive in our analysis of what Jesus actually means. If one confesses, as the church has for two millennia, that Jesus is truly God incarnate, then one simply dare not tell Jesus that his teaching is impractical in the real world and we therefore must ignore it.

Fourth, the consequences of this dualistic distinction between private and public have often been disastrous. Christians have justified their participation in terrible evil on the pretext that it is not right for them to challenge official orders. The failure of most German Protestants to oppose Hitler's atrocities is sometimes attributed in part to Luther's two-kingdom ethics. German Christians argued that "unconditional allegiance" to the Nazi state was fully compatible with allegiance to Christ.

Finally, the writings of Christians in the first three centuries clearly do not support the personal-public distinction. In every instance where they discuss killing, they say that Christians do not and should not kill. That holds in both the private realm of abortion and infanticide and also in the public realm of capital punishment and war.[3] Writing in the first decade of the fourth century, the Christian orator Lactantius insists: "God forbids us to kill. . . . Thus it will be neither lawful for a just man [a Christian] to engage in military service . . . nor to accuse anyone of a capital charge, because it makes no difference whether you put a person to death by word or rather by sword, since it is the act of putting to death itself which is prohibited."[4] Repeatedly, they reject the view that Christians may kill in the public role of soldier or executioner.

It is often argued that the Old Testament material requires some distinction between the personal and public roles with regard to murder, capital punishment, and war. (The reason cited is that the Ten Commandments forbid murder but the Old Testament repeatedly commands killing by the government in capital punishment and wars.) If that is correct, then something unusual must have happened to produce this reversal of thinking represented in the early Christian writers. They insisted that killing of every sort is wrong, both private murder by unauthorized individuals and capital punishment and war by the state. Their explanation for this radical change is Jesus. Jesus, they said, prohibits every kind of killing. Origen, probably the most widely read Christian author in the middle of the third century, explicitly discusses the distinction between the "former economy" of Israel, where killing in war was allowed, and the teaching of Christ: "For Christians could not slay their enemies or condemn to be burned or stoned, as Moses commands."[5] The most likely explanation for this significant change is that Jesus himself called his disciples to reject killing in every area of life, both private and public. That is certainly what early Christian writers thought.

QUESTIONS FOR REFLECTION AND DISCUSSION

1. How does Jesus' Sermon on the Mount teach loving enemies? And what should we conclude from his dealings with Samaritans?

2. Does Matthew 18:15-20 support a nonviolent stance? If so, how?

3. How does Jesus' discussion of the cross (for himself and his followers) relate to Jesus' call to love enemies?

4. Can you understand in your heart—really *feel*—the reasons that have moved Christians to say that Christians should sometimes kill?

5. Which arguments for why Christians should sometimes kill do you find most convincing?

6. Based on Romans 12–13, what is the central argument often used to say that Christians should sometimes kill? Do you find that argument convincing? If so, why? If not, why not?

5

Does the Rest of the New Testament Reflect What Jesus Taught?

WHAT EVIDENCE IS there that early Christianity, as represented in the New Testament beyond the Gospels, understood and carried on Jesus' teaching on peace?

Early Christianity retained the essential framework of Jewish belief and expectation—but with dramatic modifications! They embraced the Jewish belief that God had called Abraham and his descendants to be God's special people in order to bless all nations (Genesis 12:1-3). They accepted the basic Jewish understanding of a messianic time when the kingdom of God would arrive in power to defeat evil and bring dramatic transformation. But they believed that Jesus was the long-expected Messiah. They believed that in his life, death, and resurrection, Jesus had already powerfully begun (but not yet completed) the kingdom of God. That profoundly transformed their understanding. They no longer defined the kingdom in terms of the Torah's food laws, sacrifice at the temple, or an exclusive relationship with Abraham's descendants. All people are equally welcome in Jesus' new messianic kingdom. That is the framework for what the New Testament tells us about the early Christian understanding of peace.

FREQUENT USE OF THE WORD *PEACE*

That the concept of peace was important for the early church is clear simply from the widespread use of the term translated "peace" (*eirēnē*). It appears at least ninety-nine times in the New Testament. As a noun or verb, it is found at least once in every book except 1 John.

It is hardly surprising that peace became a central motif for the earliest Christians. They believed that the long-expected age of peace had actually broken into the present. Jesus the Messiah was the fulfillment of the prophetic vision of messianic shalom. In Christ, they experienced peace with God, peace with Christian brothers and sisters in the new messianic community, and inner peace of mind. The word *peace* is everywhere. So prominent is the concept of peace that early Christians sometimes describe their entire gospel message as the "gospel of peace." Again and again, Paul describes God as the "God of peace." Continually and in every way, the Lord gives peace. "Now may the Lord of peace himself give you peace *at all times in every way*" (2 Thessalonians 3:16, emphasis added).

GOD OF PEACE

This phrase, which is extremely rare in Jewish literature prior to and around the time of Jesus, is a favorite of the apostle

Paul.[1] At least six times, the New Testament writers identify God as the "God of peace" (as in Romans 15:33; 16:20; Philippians 4:9).

THE GOSPEL OF PEACE

In the story of Cornelius, Peter sums up his whole message as the "good news of peace through Jesus Christ" (Acts 10:36). In Romans 10:15, the words "those who bring good news" are from Isaiah 52:7; some ancient Greek manuscripts of Romans 10:15 (used in KJV) present have the Greek *euangelizomenōn eirēnēn* (like Isaiah 52:7). The first word is the verb form of the Greek word for "gospel." Literally, they are "evangelizing," or "gospeling." And the content of their evangelizing is the word *peace.* The meaning is that these messengers proclaim the gospel of peace.

In describing how Christ overcomes the fierce hostility between Jew and Gentile, Ephesians 2 uses the word *peace* four times. Here the word *peace* essentially becomes a word to describe the full work of salvation in Christ. And again in 2 Thessalonians 3:16, "May the Lord of peace himself give you peace at all times and in every way," the word *peace* seems to include all of salvation in Christ.

PEACE IN THE ADDRESSES OF NEW TESTAMENT LETTERS

"Grace and peace" begin almost all of Paul's letters, as well as a number of other New Testament letters.

PEACE IN THE CHURCH

Frequently the New Testament uses the word *peace* to refer to harmony in the church (Romans 14:17-19; 1 Corinthians 14:33).

"LIVE AT PEACE WITH EVERYONE"

Some places where the New Testament speaks of peace, the word seems to have a more general meaning. Romans 12:18 certainly refers to more than other Christians. It includes peace with a nonbelieving spouse (1 Corinthians 7:15).

Obviously, none of the texts just cited say anything explicit about whether Christians may ever kill. But all these texts certainly demonstrate that peace—with God, with other Christians, and with everyone—was a central concern of the entire New Testament.

PETER AND CORNELIUS

Acts 10 tells the amazing story of how a devout Jew broke important Jewish norms to preach the gospel to a Roman centurion, the visible representative of the hated national enemy. Cornelius, the centurion, lived in Caesarea, a city that typified Roman military occupation and oppression. Devout Jews like Peter would not eat with or enter the homes of Gentiles like Cornelius.

As Peter tells Cornelius the story of Jesus, he summarizes Jesus' message as the "[gospel] of peace" (Acts 10:36): "You know the message God sent to the people of Israel, announcing the good news of peace through Jesus Christ, who is Lord of all." The text here uses the same Greek construction as in some manuscripts of Romans 10:15: "evangelizing" or "proclaiming the gospel of peace" (compare Romans 10:15 [KJV]; Isaiah 52:7). Peter can summarize the whole message he brings to Cornelius as the "gospel of peace"! The full implication of this language becomes clear as one remembers not only the intense hostility between Jews and Gentiles in general but the fact that Cornelius, the Roman centurion, represents the national enemy of the Jews. Speaking to a key representative of the hated Roman imperialists, Peter says Jesus' message is a gospel of peace.

One more thing is especially significant. Augustus, the pagan Roman emperor from 27 BC to AD 14, claimed to bring the good news of peace to the world. As the bringer of "world peace"—by the sword, of course—Augustus established the worship of the goddess Pax (peace).

Peter tells a Roman centurion that Jesus, not the Roman emperor, is the Lord who brings the gospel of peace! Augustus allegedly brings peace by the sword of his successful legions. Jesus brings peace as persons embrace the cross and resurrection. But they both offer a "gospel of peace."

PEACE BETWEEN JEWS AND GENTILES

Ephesians 2:11-22 describes how peace with God, which both believing Jews and Gentiles enjoy because of the cross, effects a momentous societal peace. To even begin to understand this passage, we must realize the depth of hostility between Jews and Gentiles in the first century. Both Jewish and Gentile authors said and wrote awful things about each other.

Not surprisingly, in the first century many vicious conflicts arose between Jews and non-Jews in cities, especially in the Eastern Roman Empire. Josephus reports frequent battles in Egypt and Syria between the Jewish community and their neighbors. When one outbreak in Egypt resulted in three Jews being burned alive, the whole Jewish community threatened to burn their Gentile neighbors. And when the Jewish rebels rejected the Roman governor's appeal to calm, the governor ordered his soldiers to destroy the Jewish quarter of the city. Josephus says the Romans slaughtered fifty thousand Jews. In another place, Josephus describes the feelings of hatred or fear of their Jewish neighbors, which led to the enslavement or massacre of thousands of Jews in several Syrian cities. Clearly the hostility between Jews and Gentiles that Ephesians describes was not just theological. The two groups often despised each other, and the result was major, deadly societal violence.

The context of the Pauline teaching in Ephesians 2 is that Christ brings peace between these two warring communities. Formerly, the Gentiles were far from God, but now they "have been brought near by the blood of Christ" (v. 13). The word for "peace" is everywhere in the next five verses. Christ "himself is our peace" (v. 14). God's purpose is to create one new humanity of Jew and Gentile, "thus making peace" (v. 15). Christ preached peace to both Jews and Gentiles (v. 17).

Jesus reconciled both Jews and Gentiles to God on exactly the same basis: through the cross. As Paul says in Romans, those who receive forgiveness of sins through Christ's cross "have peace with God" (Romans 5:1, 11). Since both Jews and Gentiles are reconciled to God through the cross (Ephesians 2:16), Jews and Gentiles stand equal at the foot of the cross. And the result is peace—within the church—between the two most hostile communities in Paul's day. Jesus' cross produces "one new humanity, . . . thus making peace" (Ephesians 2:15).

It is very clear in this passage that Paul understands salvation in Christ to include vastly more than (although certainly not less than) just the forgiveness of sins and acceptance with our holy God. Salvation also includes the dramatic new social reality in the church, where Jews and Gentiles overcome their ancient hostility. In fact, in Ephesians 3 Paul goes on to discuss the "mystery" (meaning God's plan, promised to Abraham in Genesis 12:1-3, to include all people) revealed to him. And this mystery (which Paul preaches as part of the gospel!) is that Gentiles are now included in God's saving action through Israel (Ephesians 3:6).[2] And in fact this new peace, this social reconciliation of hostile groups, is so important that as the church models this new peace, it is even made known to the "rulers and authorities in the heavenly realms" (3:10). Paul uses these words to refer to the fallen angelic beings who, Paul believes, are interrelated with the distorted socioeconomic, cultural structures of our world. The new concrete social peace in the church is becoming visible well beyond the church itself.

Clearly, Jews and Gentiles were bitter enemies in Paul's day. Just as clearly, Paul announces that central to the gospel is the fact that Christ brings an astonishing new social peace between these ancient enemies. Ephesians does not have any explicit reference to Jesus' command to love our enemies. But it does provide a striking example of how Jesus' new community actually did just that.

COSMIC PEACE

According to clear indications in the New Testament, the peace that Christ brings is not limited to peace with God in forgiveness and peace with other Christians in the new social reality of the church. Colossians says both that God created all things through Christ and also that God reconciles all things through Christ: "For God was pleased to have all his fullness dwell in him, and through him to reconcile to himself all things, whether things on earth or things in heaven, by making peace through his blood, shed on the cross" (Colossians 1:19-20). The text says that this reconciliation includes the "thrones or powers or rulers or authorities" (1:16), meaning the fallen rebellious angels, originally created good, that relate to and influence the socioeconomic and cultural structures of our world. And Colossians 2:15 says Christ actually "disarmed" these "powers and authorities" at the cross. That does not mean that they are fully vanquished in this already/not yet era of Christ's dawning kingdom. The text is quite clear that these "powers and authorities" still have power and Christians must do battle with them (see Ephesians 6:12). But the victory has begun and will be completed at Christ's return. Meanwhile, the victory of Christ at the cross, a victory over these "powers and authorities," has begun to bring cosmic peace, both in heaven and on earth!

Roman citizens used the same words to speak of their emperor that Christians used for Jesus: Savior, Lord, and Son of God. The Romans used the word *gospel*, meaning "good news," to describe the military victories that ushered in the *Pax Romana*, the time of widespread peace throughout the Roman Empire. And the Romans worshiped the goddess of peace. "The concept of peace in the book of Acts," according to Princeton New Testament scholar Ulrich Mauser, "is engaged in silent dialogue with the ideal of the Roman Peace (Pax Romana)."[3]

The angry rioters in Thessalonica were not wrong when they said the Christians announced another king (Jesus) who was a rival to Caesar (Acts 17:5-8). When Peter told Cornelius, the Roman centurion, that the Christian message is a "gospel of peace" (my translation) about "Jesus Christ, who is Lord of all" (Acts 10:36), he was implicitly saying that Jesus is in charge and is the one who is truly Lord. Obviously, that means that Jesus' peace is much more than personal peace with God. The implicit message is that Jesus is also the way to societal peace.

This peace extends to the whole created order. In Romans 8:19-20, Paul says the creation (the rivers, trees, air, etc.) has been distorted by sin. But when, at the end, persons experience the resurrection of the body, then "the creation itself will be liberated from its bondage to decay and brought into the freedom and glory of the children of God" (Romans 8:21). And Revelation says that in the final consummation, "the kings of the earth will bring their splendor into" the New Jerusalem. Human civilization must be purged of its evil, but "the glory and honor of the nations will be brought into" this new city (Revelation 21:24-26).[4] Clearly Christ brings cosmic peace.

The gospel of peace that Paul preached includes much more than personal peace with God and peace in the church. This fact helps us understand the story of the riot in Thessalonica when Paul preached the gospel. Rioters dragged Paul's supporters before city officials. The charge: "They are all defying Caesar's decrees, saying that there is another king, one called Jesus" (Acts 17:7). This passage makes sense when we remember the competing claims about the Roman emperors and Jesus. Each definitely offered a different way to societal peace.

ECHOES OF JESUS

There are no New Testament passages outside the Gospels that explicitly refer to Jesus' teaching in the Sermon on the Mount. But a number of places include echoes of that sermon.

DO NOT PAY BACK WRONG FOR WRONG

At the end of 1 Thessalonians, Paul gives brief instruction on how Christians should live. "Make sure that nobody pays back wrong for wrong, but always strive to do what is good for each other and for everyone else" (5:15). That sounds like the same point as Jesus' rejection of the basic legal principle of "an eye for an eye." And Paul says Christians should live this way both in the church ("for each other") and in the larger society ("for everyone else").

WHEN CURSED, BLESS

"When we are cursed, we bless; when we are persecuted, we endure it; when we are slandered, we answer kindly" (1 Corinthians 4:12-13). Paul's instruction fits very well with Jesus' command not to respond in a hostile way to those who abuse one.

DO NOT REPAY EVIL WITH EVIL

In 1 Peter, the text seems to echo Jesus' rejection of "an eye for an eye." "Do not repay evil with evil or insult with insult. On the contrary, repay evil with blessing" (3:9).

DO NOT TAKE REVENGE

The echoes of Jesus are especially strong in Romans 12.

> Bless those who persecute you; bless and do not curse. . . . Do not repay anyone evil for evil. Be careful to do what is right in the eyes of everyone. If it is possible, as far as it depends on you, live at peace with everyone. Do not take revenge, my dear friends, but leave room for God's wrath, for it is written: "It is mine to avenge; I will repay," says the Lord. On the contrary: "If your enemy is hungry, feed him; if he is thirsty, give him something to drink. . . . Do not be overcome by evil, but overcome evil with good." (Romans 12:14-21)

Since the similarities to the Sermon on the Mount are so striking, many scholars believe that Paul knew and was using "Jesus-tradition" handed down in the church.

Paul is talking about how to respond to enemies, "those who persecute you" (v. 14). "Do not repay anyone evil for evil" (v. 17) is the same kind of restatement of Jesus' rejection of "an eye for an eye" that we have seen in 1 Thessalonians and 1 Peter. The explicit prohibition against taking revenge (v. 19) makes the same point in a slightly different way.

In Romans 12, Paul explicitly commands Christians to love our enemies, reject eye-for-eye retaliation, and forgo vengeance. That sounds very much like Jesus in the Sermon on the Mount.

IMITATING CHRIST

Again and again, throughout the New Testament, the writers insist that Christians must imitate Christ and follow him as faithful disciples. None of these texts speak specifically about whether Christians should ever kill. But this vast number of texts calling on Christians to live like Christ reinforces the claim that the rest of the New Testament has not forgotten Jesus' call to love enemies.

Christians must forgive each other "as the Lord forgave you" (Colossians 3:13; compare Ephesians 4:32). Living "as Jesus did" is the proof that one is a Christian (1 John 2:6). "We know that we have come to know him if we keep his commands" (2:3). Christians have died to their sinful selves with Christ and now share his risen life and live like him.[5] Christians should serve other Christians as Christ served them.[6] In their economic sharing with other Christians, they should imitate Christ's generosity who, "though he was rich, yet for your sake he became poor" (2 Corinthians 8:9). Christians should be humble as Christ was humble (Philippians 2:3-14).

The examples seem almost endless. "Walk in the way of love, just as Christ loved us and gave himself up for us" (Ephesians 5:2).

This call to imitate Christ is seen especially clearly in several passages calling Christians to imitate Christ in the home, the church, and socioeconomic life in the world.

IMITATING CHRIST IN THE HOME

The recipients of the letter to the Ephesians lived in a male-dominated Hellenistic society. But that does not deter the author from urging husbands to treat their wives with the same self-sacrificing love that Jesus modeled at the cross. "Husbands, love your wives, just as Christ loved the church and gave himself up for her" (Ephesians 5:25). That was a deeply radical thing to say in that society, in which women were considered greatly inferior to men. The way of the cross is not only a nonviolent way to correct injustice. It is also Christ's way of peace in the persistent struggles that batter every marriage.

THE WAY OF THE CROSS IN THE CHURCH

To illustrate the kind of humility and unselfish concern for others that Christians ought to show toward one another, Paul uses a marvelous hymn in Philippians 2:5-11: "In your relationships with one another," Paul writes, "have the same mindset as Christ Jesus." Paul's command is clear. The way to peace in the church is for Christians to allow Christ's example at the cross to be the model for their treatment of other Christians. First John 3:16 teaches the same point with equal power. That statement perfectly reflects Jesus' command to his disciples as he approached the cross: "As I have loved you, so you must love one another" (John 13:34; also 15:12). Imitating Christ at the cross is the way to peace in the church.

THE WAY OF THE CROSS IN SOCIOECONOMIC LIFE IN THE WORLD

First Peter 2 calls on Christian slaves to obey not just kind owners but also cruel masters. Christ, who suffered unjustly, is the example to imitate: "To this you were called, because Christ suffered for you, leaving you an example, that you should follow in his steps. . . . When they hurled their insults at him, he did not retaliate; when he suffered, he made no threats" (1 Peter 2:21-24).

By pondering the example of Jesus at the cross, Christians learn how to live in their socioeconomic relationships with non-Christians—and that even includes unjust oppressors. That does not mean that oppressed slaves or contemporary victims of systemic injustice should acquiesce in their oppression. In the discussion of Jesus' teaching and example, we saw that he certainly, but nonviolently, challenged and condemned evil. Yet this passage in 1 Peter clearly shows that if we obey the biblical command to follow in Christ's steps, we will refuse to regard oppressors as enemies to be reviled, hated, and destroyed. Instead, as we remember that Christ died for our sins even while we were enemies of God, we will imitate Christ's love for enemies, as demonstrated at the cross.

To say that the New Testament constantly calls Christians to imitate Christ is not to say that we are called to imitate every part of Christ's life. The New Testament does not call Christians to imitate Jesus' Jewishness, unmarried life, work as a carpenter, or once-for-all sacrifice for the sins of the world.

GOD'S LOVE FOR ENEMIES

In the discussion of Matthew 5, we saw that Jesus grounded his call to love enemies not in a naive hope that it would always produce an instant loving response but rather in the very nature of God. "Love your enemies, . . . that you may be children of your Father in heaven" (Matthew 5:44-45; also 5:9).

Probably the clearest theological expression of this teaching comes from in the apostle Paul. "God demonstrates his own love for us in this: While we were still sinners, Christ died for us. . . . While we were God's *enemies*, we were reconciled to him through the death of his Son" (Romans 5:8-10, emphasis added). Jesus' death on the cross shows that God loves his enemies.

This chapter provides abundant evidence that the earliest church, as reflected in the New Testament, did not forget or neglect Jesus' message of peace. Christ brings peace to the worst ethnic hostility in the first century, that between Jews and Gentiles. There are echoes of the Sermon on the Mount in several different places. Again and again, the New Testament calls Christians to imitate Christ—precisely at the cross. And in faithfulness to Jesus' teaching that his disciples must love their enemies in order to be children of our heavenly Father, Paul states clearly that at the cross, God loves his enemies.

QUESTIONS FOR REFLECTION AND DISCUSSION

1. What evidence is there that the earliest church embraced Jesus' teaching about peace?

2. What evidence did you find most persuasive?

3. Why is Peter's summary of the gospel in the story of Cornelius so important?

4. Does Ephesians 2–3 show that peace in the church is part of the gospel? If so, how? To what extent does your local congregation offer visible evidence of Paul's claim?

5. What evidence is there that Christ's peace includes societal peace?

6. Politicians and Jesus both claim to bring peace. How would you describe the difference?

6

But What About...?

MANY CRITICS WOULD charge that I have ignored a number of things in the New Testament that seem to support the use of violence. What about Jesus' statement that he came to bring a sword? Or the fact that there are several stories about devout soldiers and none were told to stop being soldiers? Jesus warned about wars and rumors of wars. He used a whip to cleanse the temple. Jesus even told his disciples to buy a sword. In places the New Testament seems to praise Israelite warriors and endorse the destruction of the Canaanites. Doesn't the use of military symbols endorse military action? Romans 13 certainly says that the government uses the sword to execute divine vengeance on evildoers. In fact, the New Testament says that God punishes evil, and the book of Revelation uses violent, bloody imagery to describe the final victory over evil.

Do not all these things add up to a clear endorsement of the legitimate use of killing to overcome evil?

"I CAME TO BRING A SWORD"

In Matthew 10:34, Jesus says bluntly: "I did not come to bring peace, but a sword." Christians have claimed that in this statement, Jesus endorses the violent use of the sword. But the vast majority of commentators believe that in this statement Jesus is using metaphorical language to warn his disciples that following him will invite sharp conflict in one's family, even deadly persecution.

The context supports that interpretation. In Matthew 10:16-33, just before verse 34, Jesus warns his followers that they will encounter severe persecution. And in the verses immediately following verse 34, Jesus continues to prepare his disciples for the way those who accept his message will face harsh persecution from family members (vv. 35-40).

It is clear that Luke understands Jesus' statement this way. The parallel passage in Luke 12:51 shows that Luke understood Jesus to speak of "division," not a literal sword. Jesus' words have nothing to do with his disciples using the sword. Rather, Jesus uses metaphorical language to warn his followers about severe persecution in the future.

SOLDIERS IN THE NEW TESTAMENT

There are four significant places in which the New Testament implies or states positive things about soldiers without any suggestion that they should stop being soldiers. When some soldiers respond to John the Baptist's call to repentance and ask what they should do, John responds: "Don't extort money and don't accuse people falsely—be content with your pay" (Luke 3:14-15). John does not tell them to stop being soldiers. Matthew (8:5-13) and Luke (7:1-10) include the story of the centurion who asks Jesus to heal one of his servants. When

Jesus sees the man's faith, Jesus says in amazement: "I have not found anyone in Israel with such great faith" (Matthew 8:10). Jesus says nothing about the centurion's military profession. At the cross, the Roman centurion supervising Jesus' crucifixion is the first person in Mark's gospel to say Jesus is the Son of God (15:39). And in Acts, when Peter agrees to share the gospel with a Roman centurion, the Holy Spirit falls on his household, and they are baptized (Acts 10:1–11:18). Again, the text says nothing about Peter telling the new Christian centurion that he must leave the Roman army.

For at least fifteen hundred years, prominent Christians have argued that these stories show that Jesus and the rest of the New Testament regarded the military profession as perfectly acceptable. Augustine of Hippo in the fifth century and Martin Luther and John Calvin in the sixteenth century made the same argument. So do some modern scholars. But is this claim really substantive?

At first sight, the case of John the Baptist might seem significant. Here the soldiers do ask what they are to do to respond to John's call to repentance. John specifies some things, but does not say they should stop being soldiers. But surely the precursor of Jesus does not have the same authority as Jesus. John the Baptist was not a Christian. Jesus himself clearly distinguished the time of John from the time of Jesus and Jesus' inauguration of the messianic kingdom. For Christians, Jesus and not John the Baptist provides the norms for Christian discipleship.

Second, to argue that Jesus and Peter thought that being a soldier was fine because neither story condemns the centurions' military life is to make an argument from silence. It is just as plausible to argue that Jesus and Peter told the centurions to stop being soldiers as it is to argue that Jesus and Peter said their continuing as soldiers was quite ethical. The texts say absolutely nothing about either. Both arguments are arguments from silence and, as such, carry no weight.

We know from many sources that Roman army life was immersed in pagan religion. A Roman centurion would necessarily be involved in the Roman army's pagan religious activity. The accounts of Jesus' and Peter's interactions with the centurions also say nothing about telling them to stop such pagan activity. But surely we should not conclude from this silence that Jesus and Peter thought participating in pagan religious activities was acceptable. Neither text is talking either about participating in pagan worship or participating in the army. And neither text tells us anything about whether either activity is acceptable for Jesus' disciples.

In the stories of Jesus' and Peter's encounters with the centurions, it is very clear that the focus of both stories is the amazing new reality that Jesus' dawning kingdom includes not only Jews but also Gentiles—even national enemies! The fact that both stories affirm the *faith* of centurions does not mean that Jesus and Peter are endorsing a military career any more than Jesus' praise of tax collectors and prostitutes (because they are embracing his kingdom more than many other Jews—see Matthew 21:31) means that Jesus affirms extortionate tax farming and prostitution.

Some have argued that since Jesus and some writers of the New Testament advocate paying Roman taxes, which of course helped fund the Roman army, they were affirming the validity of the military. But Roman taxes also funded pagan worship and vicious gladiatorial games where gladiators fought to the death to amuse vast audiences. If the argument that paying taxes and thus funding soldiers means the New Testament affirms the military profession, the same argument means that the New Testament affirms pagan worship and gladiatorial contests.

CLEANSING THE TEMPLE

All four Gospels describe an incident in which Jesus entered the temple, overturned the money changers' tables, and "drove out all who were buying and selling there" (Matthew 21:12; compare Mark 11:15-17; Luke 19:45-46; John 2:13-17). This is commonly called the "cleansing of the temple." Only John mentions a whip that Jesus used, at least on the animals being sold for sacrifice (John 2:15). Some Christians cite this incident as proof that Jesus used violence.

There are, however, very strong reasons for thinking that Jesus' cleansing of the temple was a brief action of dramatic symbolism, not a violent attempt to take over the temple by force.

For one thing, there were two armed forces in the immediate vicinity of the temple that would have quickly intervened if Jesus had initiated a violent attempt to seize the temple. The Jewish authorities controlled the temple police (who arrested Jesus at night a few days later). And connected to the temple by a broad staircase was the Fortress Antonia, where a Roman cohort of five to six hundred soldiers was stationed. Any substantial tumult would have certainly led to prompt intervention by one or both of those armed groups. In all three synoptic gospels, it is quite clear that Jesus continued to teach in the temple courts for several days after this incident without anyone arresting him.

All four Gospels use the same Greek verb (*ekballō*) to describe what Jesus did. The *Greek-English Lexicon of the New Testament* shows that this word can mean "throw out more or less forcibly" or "send out without the connotation of force." Mark uses this word to describe Jesus' dismissing the mourners before he heals the little girl who had died (Mark 5:40). In Matthew, the word is used to speak of the Lord sending more workers into the harvest (Matthew 9:38). In Mark 1:12, the same word is used to say that the Spirit "sent" Jesus into the wilderness to be tempted. Obviously, this word does not necessarily carry any connotation of violence.

But John 2:15 uses this word in connection with Jesus using a whip. Some translations of the Greek suggest that Jesus used the whip on the money changers as well as the animals. The problem is that the Greek text does not say that. The Good News Translation has the proper translation of the Greek: "[Jesus] drove all the animals out of the Temple, both the sheep and the cattle [or oxen]." In this incident, Jesus is far from being passive. But nothing in the text says he used the whip on the people.

In all the accounts, Jesus' words help explain his actions. After overturning the tables of the money changers, Jesus taught them saying: "Is it not written: 'My house will be called a house of prayer for all nations'? But you have made it a 'den of robbers'" (Mark 11:17; citing Isaiah 56:7 and Jeremiah 7:11). Commentators believe that the incident occurred in the outer part of the temple court reserved for Gentiles. Commercial use of the court of the Gentiles for money changers began shortly before the time of Jesus. Jesus surely felt that this commercial use of the area for the Gentiles violated the fact that the dawning kingdom would be for Gentiles as well as Jews. He probably also opposed the monopoly in monetary exchange and trade that the high-priestly families had in the temple.

Jesus' actions constituted a dramatic act of prophetic protest designed to challenge conduct that Jesus rejected. But Jesus did not even use the whip on people, much less kill them. Apparently Jesus engaged in a short symbolic, nonviolent action and then returned to his teaching. This story demonstrates the coercive power of moral authority. But it in no way supports the use of violence, much less killing.

"BUY A SWORD"

Luke (and only Luke) includes a conversation between Jesus and his disciples after the Last Supper and before their arrival at the garden of Gethsemane. After reminding the disciples that he earlier had sent them out without purse or sandals, Jesus says:

> "But now if you have a purse, take it, and also a bag; and if you don't have a sword, sell your cloak and buy one. It is written: 'And he was numbered with the transgressors'; and I tell you that this must be fulfilled in me. Yes, what is written about me is reaching its fulfillment."
> The disciples said, "See, Lord, here are two swords."
> "That's enough," he replied. (Luke 22:36-38)

Some Christians argue that this passage decisively shows Jesus as not a pacifist. In preparing them for their future dangerous missionary journeys, they say, Jesus is telling his disciples to arm themselves with swords for self-defense.

This literal understanding of the incident, however, is puzzling at several points. If Jesus intends to order his disciples to prepare themselves for self-defense on their future missionary journeys, then it is absurd for Jesus to say two swords are enough. How could two swords be adequate for even twelve disciples?

Furthermore, just a few hours later, after Peter actually uses a sword in a futile attempt to prevent Jesus' arrest, Jesus promptly rebukes him. And a few hours after that, Jesus explicitly tells Pilate that his followers do not fight (John 18:36). These actions make it highly doubtful that Jesus intended his words about buying a sword to be taken literally as a general affirmation of violent self-defense.

Two different credible explanations of this passage are proposed by scholars. The first involves a literal understanding with a very narrow specific application. The second and more common view sees Jesus' words as figurative. But in neither case does the incident mean that Jesus wanted his disciples to arm themselves for self-defense.

The first explanation starts with what Jesus said immediately after telling the disciples to buy a sword. As an apparent explanation for his command, Jesus cites Isaiah 53:12, saying that he must fulfill this passage: he must be "numbered with the transgressors." This passage in Isaiah comes at the end of a long depiction of a nonviolent, suffering servant who dies for the sin of the people. N. T. Wright says Jesus understood his calling in light of this passage. Jesus understood his death as a central part of his mission and had repeatedly predicted his death on a cross. But the Romans were the only ones with the authority to crucify people. Jesus would have known that possessing swords would make it more probable that the Roman authorities would crucify him as a likely revolutionary. Perhaps, therefore, Jesus wanted to have his disciples carry swords at his arrest. Two swords would be ridiculously inadequate for actual armed defense, but they would be enough for conviction as a revolutionary.

Most commentators, however, think Jesus' command about buying a sword was intended as a figurative way to tell his disciples that a time of severe persecution was about to descend upon them. Jesus wants to warn his disciples of impending disaster, but the disciples misunderstand his words. So he abruptly ends the conversation. Even John Calvin thought the disciples misunderstood Jesus.

One writer examined ten highly respected commentators on this passage. Many were not pacifists, but nine of the ten understood Jesus' words in a figurative way, not a call to armed defense.

PRAISE OF MILITARY LEADERS

Stephen, Paul, and the book of Hebrews all refer positively to Old Testament military events or leaders (Acts 7:45; 13:17-19; Hebrews 11). These texts, some writers argue, prove that the New Testament authors believe killing in battle to be legitimate for Christians.

But that is to claim much more than the texts say. The whole focus of Hebrews 11 is on faith in God, not the legitimacy of Christians fighting military battles. The list of heroes of faith also includes the "prostitute Rehab" (v. 31). The text says nothing about whether being a prostitute is good or evil. The same is true of the mention of the military leaders. In every case, it is their faith that is affirmed. Praising the faith of military leaders does not show that the author approves of their lethal violence any more than praising the faith of the prostitute means that the writer endorses prostitution.

Stephen and Paul are Jews. Like Jesus, they believe that God had acted to select the descendants of Abraham as his special chosen people and had given them a land so they could be

God's special instruments of revelation—a history of revelation that would culminate in Jesus' dawning messianic kingdom. In neither text is Stephen or Paul discussing whether Christians should kill or even how Christians should understand the Israelites' killing of the Canaanite men, women, and children. To argue that Stephen's and Paul's sermons justify Christian participation in war is simply to read into the text what the text does not say.

MILITARY SYMBOLS IN THE NEW TESTAMENT

Paul urges Christians to "wage war" (2 Corinthians 10:3-4) and put on "the full armor of God" (Ephesians 6:11-16). He urges Timothy to "fight the good fight of the faith" (1 Timothy 6:12; also 2 Timothy 4:7). Some Christians conclude that the New Testament's use of military symbols suggests that Christian participation in war is legitimate.

But Paul also draws an analogy between being drunk with wine and being filled with the Spirit (Ephesians 5:18). Likewise, Jesus draws analogies between himself and a thief in the night (Matthew 24:43) and between God and an unjust judge (Luke 18:1-8). No one would suppose, however, that he was recommending nocturnal thieving or judicial corruption.

A quick exploration of Paul's use of military symbols shows how he explicitly says that Christians do not fight the way the world does (2 Corinthians 10:3-4; Ephesians 6:11-17). Trying to justify war on the basis of military metaphors ignores the rules of literary interpretation.

DID JESUS ENDORSE CAPITAL PUNISHMENT?

In Matthew 15, Jesus responds to Pharisees who accuse him of breaking the tradition of the elders. In response, Jesus accuses his critics of devising legal technicalities to circumvent the clear teaching of the commandment "For God said, 'Honor your father and mother' and 'Anyone who curses their father or mother is to be put to death'" (Matthew 15:4-5). According to some interpreters, this passage demonstrates that Jesus clearly believes in capital punishment.

Two comments are important. First, Jesus does not cite the commandment to honor parents in order to comment on the validity of executing children who curse their parents. Rather, Jesus cites the commandment to critique the Pharisees for devising technicalities that allowed children to ignore their financial obligations to their parents (Matthew 15:5-6). Jesus' comments say nothing about whether he supports capital punishment for children who curse their parents.

Furthermore, in the one case in the Gospels where Jesus is asked about a situation where the Mosaic law prescribes capital punishment, Jesus very clearly does not support that action (John 7:53–8:11).

ROMANS 13

Romans 13:1-7 is probably the most widely used text to argue that God wants Christians to participate in justly authorized governmental killing.

Let everyone be subject to the governing authorities, for there is no authority except that which God has established. The authorities that exist have been established by God. Consequently, whoever rebels against the authority is rebelling against what God has instituted, and those who do so will bring judgment on themselves. For rulers hold no terror for those who do right, but for those who do wrong. Do you want to be free from fear of the one in authority? Then do what is right and you will be commended. For the one in authority is God's servant for your good. But if you do wrong, be afraid, for rulers do not bear the sword for no reason. They are God's servants, agents of wrath to bring punishment on the wrongdoer. Therefore, it is necessary to submit to the authorities, not only because of possible punishment but also as a matter of conscience. This is also why you pay taxes, for the authorities are God's servants, who give their full time to governing. Give to everyone what you owe them: If you owe taxes, pay taxes; if revenue, then revenue; if respect, then respect; if honor, then honor. (Romans 13:1-7)

In the immediately preceding verses, Paul tells the Roman Christians, in words that seem to echo Matthew 5, that they should "bless those who persecute you. . . . Do not repay anyone evil for evil. . . . Do not take revenge" (12:14-19). But then in chapter 13, Paul says that God has ordained government to punish evildoers.

Many Christians argue that the two sets of statements, taken together, mean that in their personal lives, Christians should never use lethal violence. But in their roles as public officials, they rightly participate in justly authorized killing. The Old Testament condemned an individual taking vengeance into his own hands, but clearly authorized governmental killing in capital punishment and war. Paul, it is said, assumes the same distinction and clearly intends to authorize Christian participation in justly authorized killing by the government.

How valid is this argument? Almost all scholars today recognize that Romans 12:14–13:10 is one extended argument. It is also widely recognized that Romans 12, in its strong statements about Christians rejecting revenge and vengeance, contains reminiscences of the sayings of Jesus. Paul commands Christians: "Bless those who persecute you" (v. 14). "Do not repay anyone evil for evil" (v. 17). "Do not take revenge, my dear friends, but leave room for God's wrath, for it is written, 'It is mine to avenge; I will repay,' says the Lord" (v. 19). On the contrary: "If your enemy is hungry, feed him. . . . Overcome evil with good" (vv. 20-21).

But then in the very next verse Paul says every person should "be subject" to the governing authorities. It is crucial to understand the meaning of the verb "be subject" (*hypotassesthai*) in verses 1 and 5. This term is often wrongly translated as "obey." There are, in fact, three perfectly good Greek words used in the New Testament that mean "obey," but Paul does not use any of them here. The word that Paul does use means "to be subject" (as in KJV, NIV, NRSV). One can be subject to an authority and still refuse to obey evil commands. The early Christians were quite clear that when the government commanded evil things, they had to obey God rather than human authorities (Acts 4:18-20; 5:29).

Paul goes on to list a number of things that being subject to government involves. It means not rebelling against government. It does mean paying taxes and offering respect and honor (Romans 13:6-7). But nowhere does Paul say anything about the responsibility of his readers to participate in the government's punishment of wrongdoers. Paul recognizes that government does that, and when it does so, it is a servant of God (v. 4). But nowhere does the text say that Paul's readers are to do that. In fact, immediately after the section on government, Paul returns to the theme of love, insisting that "love does no harm to a neighbor" (13:8-10).

A comparison of the Greek words in 12:19 and 13:4 demonstrates that the government does precisely the things that Paul has just commanded Christians never to do. In chapter 12, Paul says that seeking to live at peace with everyone means "Do not take revenge [*ekdikountes*], . . . but leave room for God's wrath" (*orgē*). Christians must forsake vengeance. Then in 13:4, Paul employs exactly the same words (just used to describe what Christians should *not* do) to speak about what the state does! Rulers "are God's servants, agents of wrath [*ekdikos eis orgēn*: literally, an avenger for the purpose of wrath] to bring punishment on the wrongdoer." Paul uses exactly the same words for vengeance and wrath in both places. The comment by the evangelical scholar F. F. Bruce seems correct: "The state thus is charged with a function which has been *explicitly forbidden* to the Christian."[1]

The evangelical New Testament scholar Ben Witherington concludes that Romans 13 "says absolutely nothing about Christians participating in government activities such as war or police actions."[2]

One further point about Romans 13 is important. The text clearly says that God uses government to restrain evil. But the text never says God wants government to do all the things it does or that God approves of all the things government does.

Paul embraces the typical Jewish understanding that all governmental power ultimately comes from God, who works in history to achieve God's purposes. Yet such belief does not mean that God wills or approves of all that political rulers do. Jesus told Pilate that his power came from God (John 19:11), but that does not mean that God approved of Pilate's unjust decision about Jesus. Again and again, the Old Testament says God uses pagan rulers (see Isaiah 13:3-5; 10:5-11). But God clearly disapproved of some of their actions (10:12). Nor did

Paul think that God approved when the Roman authorities persecuted Christians. Nothing in the text suggests that Paul thinks that God approves of all the actions of the governing authorities, which God somehow "establishes." The text does not even say that God wants government to execute vengeance via the sword. It simply says that government does so, and God uses officials to restrain evil.

SINCE GOD "KILLS GOD'S ENEMIES . . ."

Some Christians argue that since God punishes and ultimately in some sense kills sinners, therefore the claim that Christians should never kill collapses. The teaching about final judgment and the eternal departure of sinners from God clearly appears frequently in the New Testament. Paul speaks of it repeatedly (as in Acts 17:30-31; 2 Corinthians 5:10-11; Romans 2:5-8). Jesus himself, the teacher of love, says as much or more about eternal separation from God as any other part of the New Testament does (see Matthew 13:41-42; 18:8; 25:41).

But does the fact that God punishes sinners mean that Christians are authorized to kill? Romans 12:14-21 says both that Christians should not seek revenge or repay evil for evil and also that God does that! Paul is clearly teaching that God will do what Christians should not do.

God is different from human beings. It is true that the Bible often commands believers to imitate God. But not at every point. Human beings do not create *ex nihilo* or die for the sins of the world. And the New Testament explicitly teaches that Christians should not imitate God in God's exercise of vengeance and killing. Only the One who is the perfect combination of love and justice, mercy and holiness, knows enough to do that rightly.

Therefore, to point out that Jesus seems to recognize and approve of God's destruction of Sodom or the flood in Noah's day says nothing about whether Christians should kill. The same is true of the death of Ananias and Sapphira in Acts 5:1-11. The text simply does not say that Peter killed them for lying. The clear, although unstated, implication is that God chose to punish them immediately. The New Testament explicitly tells Christians not to do some things that the all-knowing God rightly does.

I believe that both theodicy and nonviolence require God's ultimate suppression of evil. Justice seems to demand a final judgment, where God deals with evil. The assurance of a final judgment upon evil and evildoers is also a crucial foundation of nonviolence. "Without entrusting oneself to the God who judges justly, it will hardly be possible to follow the crucified Messiah and refuse to retaliate when abused. The certainty of God's just judgment at the end of history is the presupposition for the renunciation of violence in the middle of it."[3]

To say that in the end some people depart eternally from God is not a claim that God preserves some people in conscious existence in order to punish them eternally. I am inclined to understand eternal separation from God as the result of God taking our freedom so seriously that God (with immeasurable sorrow) allows people to reject his offer of loving forgiveness so long that they cease to exist.

REVELATION'S VIOLENT IMAGERY

The famous nineteenth-century atheist Friedrich Nietzsche called the last book of the Bible "the most rabid outburst of vindictiveness in all recorded history."[4] Without question, there is violent imagery in Revelation. It depicts Jesus as riding on a white horse, with eyes "like blazing fire" as he "wages war" against all who follow the antichrist (19:11-21).

Some Christians conclude that Revelation supports Christian use of violence. But such a view ignores a great deal about this unique book, full of strange, powerful imagery.

Modern scholars recognize that the book was probably written around the reign of Emperor Domitian (AD 81–96). Christians were suffering persecution by Rome. The book's central message is that Christians should remain faithful to Christ even if they are martyred (2:10) because Christ is now "King of kings and Lord of lords" (19:16). He will eventually conquer all evil.

Jesus is the center of Revelation. And the most significant statement about Jesus is that he is the "slaughtered lamb." That image of Christ appears twenty-eight times in the book! It appears first in chapter 5, where John laments the fact that no one seems able to open the scroll with the seven seals. But one of the elders assures John that the "Lion of the tribe of Judah" (5:5) can open it. Language about the lion of the tribe of Judah reflects the widespread Jewish expectation for a conquering military messiah. But when the lion appears, he is "a Lamb looking as if it had been slain" (v. 6)! John says this slaughtered lamb stands at the center of the throne of God. Everywhere in Revelation, Jesus is the slain Lamb. Using this language, Revelation rejects the idea of a militaristic messiah and explains that the true Messiah conquers evil with suffering love.

The message is clear. God is now dealing with the world through the cross of Christ. Jesus is now conquering Rome through his cross as the slain Lamb. Just as definitely, Revelation says that Christians conquer Satan by suffering, not fighting: "They triumphed over him by the blood of the Lamb and the word of their testimony; they did not love their lives so much as to shrink from death" (12:11). They conquered by dying, just as Christ had done (also 2:10-11).

It is true that the martyred Christians depicted in Revelation long for an end to their suffering (6:10). Yet that longing reflects the common New Testament teaching that God will eventually deal with evil. But, as the epistles say (Romans 12:19; 2 Thessalonians 1:6-8; 1 Peter 2:23), God is the one who does vengeance, not people.

The book of Revelation clearly teaches what Jesus also taught: a final judgment (20:11-15). Before that final judgment, Christ the Lamb powerfully conquers all evil. Some of the imagery used to describe that battle is violent. But one should probably not read those words in a literal way. Revelation is apocalyptic literature, which uses vivid symbols to describe basic truths.[5] And the essential idea is that, in the end, God will conquer all evil.

Nowhere does Revelation say that the saints fight in this final battle. The "armies of heaven" that follow the rider on the white horse (19:14) are not human beings. Repeatedly, Revelation says that the saints suffer, even up to death. But it never says they fight back. In fact, 13:10 tells them not to use the sword. Not even in the final battle against evil do human beings participate. At the end, as in the middle of history, vengeance is something that God, not God's people, enacts.

Over the ages some Christians have used the texts and incidents discussed in this chapter to argue that, according to the New Testament, sometimes Christians should kill. But the arguments are weak and strained. They are never convincing. Careful examination of these passages confirms the view that the New Testament consistently teaches Christians never to kill.

QUESTIONS FOR REFLECTION AND DISCUSSION

1. Which challenges to pacifism and nonviolence do you consider most compelling?

2. Which challenges are least convincing?

3. Where do you find the author's responses convincing? Where are they inadequate?

4. Are there other challenges that should be considered? What are they? How would you respond?

7

Jesus and Killing in the Old Testament

WHAT ABOUT ALL the divine commands to kill in the Old Testament? There are scores of passages that say God commanded God's people to kill others. Does that not mean that sometimes Christians should do the same today?

All Christians agree that the one God of the universe is revealed most fully in Jesus of Nazareth: true God and true man. And Jesus tells us to love our enemies "that you may be children of your Father in heaven" (Matthew 5:44-45). Did that same God repeatedly command the people of Israel to slaughter every man, woman, and child in city after city? Did that same God command capital punishment for lazy children or those who gathered sticks on the Sabbath?

THE VIOLENT TEXTS

The Old Testament again and again says that God commanded the Israelites to obliterate every living person in the towns they captured: "Do not leave alive anything that breathes. Completely destroy them" (Deuteronomy 20:16-17). Joshua 10 describes Joshua conquering city after city: "The city and everyone in it Joshua put to the sword. He left no survivors there" (Joshua 10:30; also vv. 32, 35, 37, 39). And after relating Joshua's victory over the whole region, the Bible declares: "He left no survivors. He totally destroyed all who breathed, just as the Lord, the God of Israel, had commanded" (v. 40).

These texts reflect Israel's holy war tradition of *hērem* (setting something apart for destruction). A Moabite inscription from the ninth century BC reflects the same practice of slaughtering all the captives of a city defeated in battle as a sacrifice to one's god for giving victory in battle. This genocidal practice (often commanded by Yahweh) appears thirty-seven times in the Old Testament. Apparently Israel understood such slaughtering of every man, woman, and child in a defeated Canaanite city as an act of worship to Yahweh (Joshua 6:21).

The Old Testament also depicts God as commanding death for a wide range of things: adultery (Leviticus 20:10); lighting a fire or gathering sticks on the Sabbath (Exodus 31:14; 35:2-3; Numbers 15:32-36); children who are stubborn, lazy, or drunkards (Deuteronomy 21:18-21; Exodus 21:15, 17; Leviticus 20:9); cursing God (Leviticus 24:16); sacrificing to an idol (Exodus 22:20). The Bible says that Yahweh sent an angel to slaughter seventy thousand Israelites because King David took a census (2 Samuel 24:15). Some psalms portray God and God's people as engaged in or anticipating vicious actions (for example, Psalm 68:22-23; 137:8-9). Judges 20 tells how the other tribes went to war against the tribe of Benjamin and—at the command of God—slaughtered 25,100 Benjamites (Judges 20:18-25). In more than a hundred biblical passages, Yahweh commands people to kill other persons.

How can all this Old Testament material in which God commands killing, war, the slaughtering of every man, woman, and child, thus indeed genocide, be reconciled with God's final revelation in Jesus that God wants us to love our enemies? Many Jews in Jesus' day longed for another "holy war" when their God would again destroy the national enemy, this time the Roman conquerors. But Jesus totally rejected that approach. The contrast between Moses's final words to his people and Jesus' final words to his disciples can hardly be more stark. Moses told his people to enter the land and do to the Canaanites "all that I have commanded you" (Deuteronomy 31:1-5). Jesus' final command was to go into the whole world and make disciples of all nations, teaching them "to obey everything that I have commanded you" (Matthew 28:19-20). And that included loving their enemies!

JESUS AND THE OLD TESTAMENT

An easy solution, of course, would be to reject all these Old Testament texts. They are merely ancient documents reflecting ghastly primitive ideas that have no authoritative relevance for New Testament Christians. But the same Lord Jesus who taught his disciples to love their enemies clearly shared the first-century Jewish and then Christian view that "all scripture is God-breathed" (2 Timothy 3:16). In the story of his temptation by Satan (Matthew 4; Luke 4), Jesus responds to each of Satan's three temptations with "It is written," and then cites a text from Deuteronomy. (In Jewish circles of Jesus' day, the phrase "It is written" was commonly used to introduce the Hebrew Bible). And near the beginning of the

Sermon on the Mount, Jesus states his commitment to the "Law" and "the Prophets": "Until heaven and earth disappear, not the smallest letter, not the least stroke of a pen, will by any means disappear from the Law until everything is accomplished" (Matthew 5:17-18; compare also Mark 12:36; Luke 24:44).

Clearly Jesus thought and taught that the Law, Psalms, and Prophets were the authoritative Word of God. If we confess that Jesus is true God and true man, then we dare not dismiss his teaching about the Hebrew Bible.

In a variety of different ways, many contemporary scholars do something of that sort. One recent scholar proposes commonly accepted modern standards of morality as a good standard for judging what the Bible says. The standard is what "any mentally healthy, rationally functioning human being should quickly and easily recognize" as right or wrong.[1] But it is not obvious that Jesus' command to love our enemies would fare much better with this standard than Old Testament texts on violence! For those who confess Jesus as Lord, some widely accepted, modern ethical norms dare not provide our fundamental ethical criteria.

PROPOSED SOLUTIONS

There have been various attempts to justify or at least soften the texts that describe the slaughter of everything that breathes in the Canaanite cities that the Israelites reportedly conquered. These include: It never happened. God promised the land to Israel. The Canaanites were wicked. The pagan Canaanites would have corrupted the people of Israel if they had remained in the land. All Near Eastern nations of that day did the same thing. Perhaps the language about killing everything that breathes represents a widely used literary form that greatly exaggerates the amount of killing. Since God chose to reveal himself to a nation and warfare was essential to the survival of any nation, warfare was necessary. Let's examine each of these.

IT NEVER HAPPENED

Archaeologists have done extensive excavations in the area of the cities allegedly totally destroyed according to Joshua 6–11. Only seven of the twelve cities reportedly destroyed by Joshua were even occupied at the time. And only three show signs of destruction at the time of the alleged conquest. Conclusion? The total destruction of the Canaanites never happened. But even if these archaeologists are right, it does not remove the theological problem: these biblical texts—which are part of the God-breathed authoritative Scripture, according to Jesus—say that God ordered the annihilation of all that breathed.

GOD PROMISED THE LAND TO ABRAHAM'S DESCENDANTS

Both testaments tell us that God chose to give land to Abraham's descendants, to bless all nations (Genesis 12:1-3)—a plan fulfilled in Jesus. Does that mean that the only way almighty God could have accomplished this plan was to slaughter every Canaanite living there?

WICKED CANAANITES

It is true that the Canaanites were wicked. They worshiped idols, sacrificed their children to their gods, and practiced cult prostitution (Genesis 15:16; Exodus 23:33; Leviticus 18:1-3, 27-28; Deuteronomy 9:4). But again, we must ask, Is genocide the only way to punish such sinners?

OTHER NEAR EASTERN NATIONS DID IT

We know from extrabiblical documents that slaughtering all the inhabitants of a defeated city was not uncommon at this time in history. But does this widespread practice by pagans justify God's alleged command to *Israel* to do the same?

HYPERBOLIC LANGUAGE

Some scholars point out that many Near Eastern documents of this period show that the kings of the day regularly used highly hyperbolic language to overstate the extent of killing resulting from their military campaigns. In Joshua the language of wiping out everything that breathes is strikingly similar to other ancient accounts of military victories. So the killing reported in some biblical texts was probably not intended to be taken literally and was not really as extensive as the texts seem to imply. Furthermore, the book of Judges frequently describes battles against Canaanites who the book of Joshua says have already been obliterated (compare Joshua 10–11 with Judges 1:1-2; 5). Conclusion? The final editor of the books of Joshua and Judges was not even intending to imply that Joshua literally slaughtered all that breathed.

How much does this argument help? Not much. If the final editor did not think that God or Moses commanded the slaughter of all that breathes, then it is strange that the same editor repeatedly included language explicitly stating that God and Moses *did command exactly that.* Thus we are still left with the fact that the biblical texts repeatedly say that God commanded genocide. I find it very difficult to think that the Father of our Lord Jesus would actually do that.

YODER'S EXPLANATION

John Howard Yoder tried to understand these hard texts while advocating a canonical approach that seeks to accept the full canon as an authoritative Word of God.[2] He rejected several common approaches. Dispensationalists said a sovereign God commands different things in different dispensations. That approach seems to compromise Jesus' teaching that he is the fulfillment of Israelite faith. Was war in the Old Testament perhaps a concession to disobedience in the way Moses allowed divorce because of the hardness of people's hearts? Yoder rejected this approach because the idea of concession to disobedience is not in the texts on holy war. Nor did Yoder accept the idea that the texts on killing in the Old Testament come from a "primitive moral immaturity" that our more civilized culture rightly rejects. It is problematic, Yoder insisted, because this position seems to derive from "an evolutionist liberal theological perspective" that he did not share. And Yoder also rejected the widespread view that the Old Testament distinction between private and public responsibility (the individual should not kill on one's own initiative, but the state rightly does so) also applies in the New Testament. Yoder rejected this approach, which claims that Jesus' rejection of killing applies only to one's private life, not one's public life as citizen and soldier.

Yoder's approach seeks to embrace what the biblical text says in its story of the history of Israel. And within that history, he finds a progressive direction, where the sacredness of human life is increasingly protected.

God called Abraham out of a violent culture. The texts on Israel's movement into Canaan call on Israel to trust in God's miraculous intervention, not their own military power. When Israel demands a king to lead them into battle, God's prophet opposes the idea and warns the king not to trust in military power. The later prophets repeatedly condemned the kings for trusting in military preparedness rather than God's protection. And these later prophets announced that a time will come when all people, not just Abraham's physical descendants, will be part of God's people—a promise fulfilled in Jesus, who taught his followers to love all people, even their enemies.

There is obvious merit in Yoder's argument. He accepts the Old Testament as part of God's authoritative revelation. Jesus is the fulfillment of God's promise to bless all nations through Abraham's descendants. There is a development within the Old Testament.

But Yoder's argument still affirms that God did command the people of Israel to slaughter everything that breathed in the conquered Canaanite cities.[3] This means that God commanded genocide. Must we accept that the Father of our Lord Jesus commanded something so utterly contradictory to what Jesus himself taught?

It is true, as John Nugent argues in his exposition of Yoder's understanding of the Old Testament, that Jesus' teaching on loving enemies does not represent "an exhaustive representation of God's response to evil." According to explicit teaching in the New Testament, God does some things that Christians must not (Romans 12:19). Furthermore, as Yoder argues, finite human beings have no adequate way to judge whether the actions of the infinite God are morally justified. Since there is an "infinite qualitative distinction" between God and human beings, we have no criteria for judging what would be right for God to do. "We cannot be certain that divine sanction of genocide is a contradiction unless we have a firm grasp on the nature of divinity which we lack."[4]

But that still seems profoundly inadequate. It surely is a mistake to argue that Jesus *totally* reveals everything about God. And Jesus repeatedly teaches that God punishes evil. God properly does some things that Jesus' disciples are commanded not to do. But Jesus does tell us that when we love our enemies, we act like God, who sends the rain on the just and unjust. Is genocide compatible with the loving God whom Jesus describes?

BOYD'S EXPLANATION

Gregory A. Boyd believes that we must answer "no" to that question. And in his massive two-volume *Crucifixion of the Warrior God*, Boyd tries to develop a way to reconcile Jesus' call to nonviolence with Jesus' belief in the Old Testament as the authoritative Word of God.

We must start with Jesus. In many different places and ways, the New Testament says what is very clear in Hebrews.[5] The Law and Prophets are inferior to Jesus in the way a shadow is inferior to the substance (Hebrews 10:1; 8:5; Colossians 2:17). The New Testament authors read the Old Testament in light of Jesus, and we must do the same. Jesus is the center of the Bible, and the cross is the center of Jesus.

Whenever an Old Testament text depicts God in a way that corresponds to God as revealed at the cross, it is a direct revelation that we must accept. But when an Old Testament passage describes a violent God, which does not conform to the nonviolent God revealed at the cross, it is the human author expressing wrong, sinful ideas that we must reject.

How adequate is Boyd's solution? I find many commendable things in his massive, 1,400-page, magnum opus.[6] He is right to start with Jesus as God's fullest revelation to us. He is right to show the numerous ways Jesus and the New Testament fulfill the Law and the Prophets by modifying or setting aside numerous Old Testament demands—whether food laws, the Sabbath, circumcision, and so on. But in the end, it is not clear that his position differs substantively from those modern authors who judge that the Old Testament is wrong. Boyd's approach is certainly vastly more complex than many others. But in the end, he says that whenever the Old Testament depicts a violent God, we are dealing with sinful, misguided human authors.

OTHER OLD TESTAMENT TEXTS

It is simply not the case that Old Testament texts depicting God as commanding or doing violence provide the only picture of who God is. There are many texts, perhaps even more texts, that describe God's overflowing love. In Exodus, God describes himself as "the compassionate and gracious God, slow to anger, abounding in love and faithfulness, . . . forgiving wickedness, rebellion and sin" (34:6-7). The description of God as "slow to anger, abounding in love" appears again and again in the Old Testament (Numbers 14:18; Nehemiah 9:17; Psalm 86:15; 103:8; 145:8; Joel 2:13; Jonah 4:2). One of the most common words applied to Yahweh in the Old Testament is *hesed*, which means "steadfast love." Forty-two different times, the Old Testament declares that God's "steadfast love endures forever" (as in Psalm 136). Some Old Testament passages, especially in the prophets, describe God as hating violence and bringing peace in the future (Isaiah 11:6-9; Micah 4:3). Love is central to the Old Testament depiction of who God is.

These many texts, however, do not change the fact that the Old Testament repeatedly depicts God as commanding and doing violence, even genocide. So the problem remains: How do we reconcile these texts with what Jesus tells us about God?

I am not satisfied with any of the attempts I know to understand how Old Testament passages that depict a violent God fit with Jesus' revelation of God, who calls us to love even our enemies. Perhaps, this side of eternity, no answer will seem adequate. But I do think some things are clear. We should start with Jesus. And Jesus and the New Testament fulfill many central Old Testament things—precisely by transcending and replacing them! We must start with Jesus, not the Old Testament.

THE SHADOW AND THE REALITY

Hebrews declares that the Old Testament law is but "a shadow" of the genuine reality disclosed in Jesus Christ (10:1-18). Now that Christ, the "exact representation" of God, has come, the old is set aside (Hebrews 1:3). In the new covenant, many things central to the old covenant—the law, the temple, circumcision, the Sabbath, oaths, "an eye for an eye" retaliation—are no longer normative for God's people.

Both in the teaching of the Old Testament and the belief of first-century Jews, the law and the temple were at the center of Jewish faith. Keeping the details of the law scrupulously was the way to obey Yahweh and demonstrate that one was a faithful Jew. The temple was the place where God was uniquely present and where daily sacrifices for sin were made. The early church set all that aside, believing that Jesus, not the law and the temple, was the way to God.

THE SABBATH

The Sabbath was firmly established in the Ten Commandments (Exodus 20:8) as a central feature of Jewish life (34:21). Even lighting a fire in one's home on the Sabbath merited death (35:2-3).

Jesus had repeated conflicts with the Pharisees about the Sabbath (Matthew 12:1-14). He even claimed to be "Lord of the Sabbath" (12:8), insisting that "the Sabbath was made for people, not people for the Sabbath" (Mark 2:27 TNIV).

There is no evidence that Jesus specifically rejected Sabbath observance. But the early church clearly considered it unnecessary (Romans 14:5-6). And Colossians 2 declares the Sabbath as "a shadow of the things that were to come; the reality, however, is found in Christ" (vv. 16-17)—a view, as we will see, that Paul applied to the entire Torah.

FOOD LAWS SET ASIDE

Food laws were also an important part of the Torah. The entire chapter of Leviticus 11 specifies in great detail which foods are clean and unclean. Devout Jews of Jesus' day observed the food laws scrupulously.

As Jesus taught, however, nothing that enters the body from outside can defile a person. The writer of Mark added: "In saying this, Jesus declared all foods clean" (Mark 7:17-19). Other parts of the New Testament demonstrate that keeping the Torah's food laws was no longer an obligation for God's people. The great council in Jerusalem decided that Gentile Christians did not need to keep the food laws of the Torah (Acts 15). In Romans 14, Paul says: "All food is clean" (v. 20)—a clear rejection of the Old Testament's food laws (also 1 Corinthians 10:25). Galatians 2 makes it clear that the Torah's food laws are irrelevant for both Jewish and Gentile Christians.

CIRCUMCISION IS NOTHING

Male circumcision was a central part of the Mosaic law and an important practice for first-century Jews. It was a crucial way for Jews to distinguish themselves from Gentiles. Genesis 17 specifies circumcision for Abraham's descendants as an essential sign of God's covenant. At the Jerusalem council, the early church clearly rejected the idea that Gentile Christians must be circumcised to be part of the people of God (Act 15). Paul declares circumcision as irrelevant for Jews and Gentiles (Romans 4:9-17). "Circumcision is nothing and uncircumcision is nothing" (1 Corinthians 7:19). "In Christ Jesus neither circumcision nor uncircumcision has any value" (Galatians 5:6; compare 6:15). Circumcision, so central to Old Testament faith, is irrelevant for God's new multiethnic people.

TORAH ABOLISHED

The New Testament does not merely set aside important parts of the law, such as circumcision, Sabbath, and food laws. Ephesians says that the law itself was "set aside" (NIV) or "abolished" (NRSV) in Christ (Ephesians 2:15). One grasps how radical this teaching was only when one remembers how important the law was to Old Testament life and first-century Jewish belief.

Deuteronomy says that as Moses prepared to give the "decrees and laws" to Israel, he said: "Follow them so that you may live" (Deuteronomy 4:1). In another text, God commands the people: "Keep my decrees and laws, for the person who obeys them will live by them" (Leviticus 18:5; also Deuteronomy 31; Ezekiel 20:11). In Jesus' day, Jews believed both that failure to keep the law had resulted in exile and that faithful keeping of the law would hasten the coming of the messiah.

Why, then, does Paul teach that "all who rely on the works of the law are under a curse" (Galatians 3:10)? Why does he insist that "you who are trying to be justified by the law have been alienated from Christ" (Galatians 5:4)?

In Christ, people are justified by faith. But the law, Paul insists, "is not based on faith; on the contrary, it says [quoting Leviticus 18:5], 'The person who does these things will live by them'" (Galatians 3:12). According to the law, life comes through obeying its provisions.

Paul understood the law as a "guardian," needed only until the minor reaches adulthood. "We were held in custody under the law, locked up until the faith that was to come [in Christ] would be revealed. So the law was our guardian until Christ came that we might be justified by faith. Now that this faith has come, we are no longer under a guardian" (Galatians 3:23-25). Paul is very clear. Believers in Christ—both Jew and Gentile—are "not under the law" (5:18). The law is a mere "shadow" of what is present in Christ (Colossians 2:17). Paul is setting aside not just this or that minor provision of the Old Testament but the Torah itself, which was at the very center of Old Testament faith.

THE TEMPLE REPLACED

Along with the Torah, the temple in Jerusalem was at the core of Jewish life in Jesus' day. Yahweh was uniquely present there. In the sacrificial system at the temple, Yahweh offered forgiveness and cleansing. The temple was the heart of Judaism. But Jesus somewhat indirectly and the later New Testament explicitly say that Jesus replaces the temple.

Matthew (9:2-8), Mark (2:1-12), and Luke (5:17-16) tell the story of the lame man carried to Jesus by his friends. But when Jesus forgave his sins, the religious leaders denounced it as blasphemy. Jesus' action was an indirect yet clear claim that what the temple offered was available through him—even though every good Jew knew that God forgave sins through the officially authorized channels of temple and priesthood.

Jesus' cleansing of the temple was an even more explicit claim to have authority over the temple. Jewish belief in Jesus' day understood the true, expected Davidic king to be the true ruler of the temple. Jesus had just ridden into Jerusalem in the triumphal entry, making a clear claim to be the expected messiah. Now he claims the authority to cleanse the temple. Some scholars believe that Jesus' action in the temple was not only a judgment on the temple. It was also, by implication, a claim that he himself was the new temple (compare Matthew 12:6; 26:61).

Whether or not Jesus himself claimed that he was replacing the temple, the New Testament certainly did. Hebrews 7–10 has a long discussion of Jesus as both priest (7:11-12; 9:11) and sacrifice (9:26). The true temple is in heaven, not in Jerusalem. The Jerusalem temple is only a "copy and shadow of what is in heaven" (8:5). The old sacrificial system had to be constantly repeated to cover sins. But Jesus offered himself in the true heavenly temple "once for all by his own blood, thus obtaining eternal redemption" (9:12).

A BETTER COVENANT

As Hebrews makes quite clear, Jesus has replaced everything that the temple stood for and accomplished. The old covenant prescribed regular sacrifices in the temple in Jerusalem and now is "obsolete; and what is obsolete and outdated will soon disappear" (8:13; see also 10:9). Jesus has established a "better" and "new covenant," which is "superior to the old one" (7:22; 8:6; see also 12:24). The law, the temple in Jerusalem with its sacrifice, and the old covenant are all only a "shadow" (10:1) of what we have in Christ.

Paul was at least as stark in describing the difference between the old and new covenants (2 Corinthians 3:4-11). The old covenant, "engraved in letters on stone" (v. 7), was "transitory" (v. 11) and "brought death" (v. 7) and "condemnation" (v. 9). Paul celebrated the new covenant in Christ's blood (1 Corinthians 11:23-25). The "new covenant" is far more glorious and (unlike the temporary first covenant) lasts forever (2 Corinthians 3:6, 11).

Jesus' superiority to the Law and the Prophets in the old covenant also emerges in Jesus' discussion of John the Baptist (Matthew 11:7-15). Jesus considered John the Baptist at least as great as the greatest Old Testament prophets. But then Jesus adds that "whoever is least in the kingdom of heaven is greater than he" (v. 11)—a clear implication that Jesus and his dawning kingdom transcend the Law and the Prophets (compare Matthew 11:27; John 1:17-18).

The New Testament does not say that Jesus teaches something totally new. Rather, he fulfilled God's plan all along to bless all nations through Abraham and his descendants (Genesis 12:1-3). Yet the law—with its food laws, circumcision, and strict Sabbath observance—had erected a "dividing wall of hostility" between Jew and Gentile (Ephesians 2:14). But Christ, "by setting . . . aside the law with its commands" (v. 15), enabled one new reconciled humanity of Jew and Gentile. That was the mystery of the gospel that had been "hidden for ages" (Colossians 1:26). But in fulfilling the promise of the Old Testament, Jesus and his new community transcended and set aside central aspects of the Old Testament.

It is in this context that we must understand Jesus' setting aside of the Old Testament's clear teaching on oaths and retaliation calling for "an eye for an eye"—in fact, Jesus' entire teaching and example against violence. Many devout Jews of Jesus' day fervently believed that God would keep his ancient promises to Israel by sending a military messiah who would wage violent war against the pagans, destroying them and establishing Jerusalem and a rebuilt temple as the center of the world. Jesus did claim to be the expected messiah. Jesus did believe that God was fulfilling in himself the ancient promise to Abraham to make his descendants a blessing to the whole world. But Jesus taught that loving enemies, not killing them, was God's way. Jesus insisted that children of the heavenly Father must love their enemies. And Jesus modeled that teaching all the way to the cross. Furthermore, God raised him on the third day to demonstrate that Jesus' way was God's way.

The evidence is quite clear. In both his life and his teaching, Jesus rejected the way of violence, loved his enemies, and insisted that his disciples do the same. If one confesses, as the church has for two millennia, that the teacher from Nazareth is God in the flesh, then we dare not say that Jesus was wrong. To reject Jesus' teaching on loving enemies is to deny the deity of Christ.

Christians today believe with the early Christians that Jesus Christ is God's final revelation to us. We believe that the old covenant is a mere shadow of the new covenant in Christ. We believe that the new covenant fulfills by *setting aside* central aspects (law, circumcision, temple) of the old covenant. Since we believe that, then we must start with Jesus' teaching about who God is and what God demands of God's people. To start with Old Testament statements about violence and insist that Jesus' teaching must be interpreted to fit Old Testament texts flatly contradicts the entire New Testament hermeneutic. Constantly, the New Testament understands the Old Testament through the lens of the final revelation in Christ. The former is but a shadow. The clear revelation is in

Jesus Christ the Lord. To return to the shadow is finally to deny Christ.

That still leaves me without a fully satisfactory answer to the question of how to reconcile Old Testament statements about violence with Jesus and the New Testament. Are these Old Testament statements simply misguided ideas by sinful, societally conditioned human beings? Perhaps, but I do not see how that fits with Jesus' teaching about the Old Testament as the Word of God. Did God actually command the slaughter of the Canaanites? Perhaps, and if God did, I accept the truth that finite human beings have no authority or standing to judge the Infinite One. But if Jesus was right in revealing that God is love—indeed, so profoundly love that God even submits to the terror of Roman crucifixion out of amazing, unfathomable love for sinful enemies—then I cannot see how the Father of Jesus would command genocide.

Some Old Testament prophets speak of a future messianic time when war will end and peace will prevail. We also know that some of these passages were understood in Jesus' day to refer to a coming messiah. Jesus certainly claimed to be that messiah. He taught that the messianic kingdom breaking into history means loving enemies, even vicious Roman imperialists. Thus passages in the prophets that point toward a future day when God would establish a new covenant and bring a new day when swords would be beaten into plowshares—these texts fit well with the understanding that, whatever the proper understanding of violence in the Old Testament, we now live under the new covenant, with its rejection of killing.

Perhaps this side of eternity, we will never have an adequate answer to the question of violence in the Old Testament. But that lack of clarity in no way leaves uncertain what faithful

disciples of Jesus should believe and do. If God's final revelation, the eternal Son of God, calls his disciples to love their
enemies, we must obey.

QUESTIONS FOR REFLECTION AND DISCUSSION

1. How do you and your Christian friends interpret the Old
   Testament passages about God commanding the slaughter
   of the Canaanites and others who displease God? How do
   you evaluate those interpretations?

2. Have you thought much about the implications of these
   Old Testament texts for Jesus' teaching on loving enemies?

3. Which of the solutions discussed in the text do you agree
   with or reject? Why?

4. How would you describe the author's view? What are its
   strengths and weaknesses?

5. The New Testament clearly set aside many central Old
   Testament commands and practices. Does that help you
   understand the violent Old Testament passages? How?

8

Foundational Theological Issues

WHO IS JESUS? How is Jesus' resurrection important for the discussion? What are the implications of the fact that the messianic kingdom announced by Jesus Christ has already begun but is not yet complete? How is the church important to our question? If Jesus did teach a nonviolent ethic, is it possible that it's only intended for the church or even for just some Christians? Answers to these important theological issues are essential for answering our question of whether Jesus sometimes wants his followers to use lethal violence.

WHO IS JESUS?

If classical Christian creeds are correct in confessing that Jesus is truly God and truly man, then the incarnate Son of God must be normative for Christians. Christians believe that Jesus lived a sinless life. If he is fully human and fully divine, then his teaching and sinless life disclose God's revelation of how humanity should live.

Obviously, if Jesus is not truly God, then the argument for nonviolence based on his teaching is weak. On the other hand, precisely the classical orthodox understanding of Jesus as true God and true man demands that Christians seek to submit to his teaching, including his teaching on loving enemies. To do otherwise is to imply that Jesus did not know what he was talking about, that he was mistaken in his teaching. This would be a denial of his divinity.

But that is essentially what people like Reinhold Niebuhr do. Yes, Jesus taught us to love our enemies, but Jesus' ethic does not work in the real world. This thinking proposes that responsible Christians should not try to live the ethic of love that Jesus taught.

That conclusion is simply unacceptable if, with the ancient creeds, one believes that Jesus is true God as well as true man. If the ancient creeds are correct, then orthodox Christians must seek to live what Jesus taught his disciples. Anything less represents theological heresy.

IF JESUS IS NOT RISEN . . .

The one who taught his disciples to love their enemies was crucified. The one who claimed to be the long-expected messiah—who announced that the messianic kingdom had broken into history in his person and work—experienced the ultimate human proof that his claims were false.

Every Jew in Jesus' day knew that a self-proclaimed messiah the Romans killed was not just a failure. He was also a fraud. There is no evidence from this period that followers of someone who claimed to be messiah actually continued to believe in him after he died. Except for Jesus!

The reason Jesus' disciples continued to call him Messiah after his crucifixion by the authorities was that they found his tomb empty and met the risen Jesus. His resurrection was what convinced the discouraged disciples that the messianic kingdom Jesus was announcing had truly begun, and that they should make disciples of all nations, teaching them to obey all that Jesus had taught them.[1]

Jesus' call to love enemies makes no sense if he is still in the tomb. An empty tomb, a risen Crucified One, is a central, necessary foundation of any claim that followers of Jesus should refuse to kill.

But the resurrection definitely does not guarantee the immediate success of nonviolent action. Throughout the ages, starting with Stephen, Christian martyrs loved their enemies, but they were killed and they stayed dead! It is only when one grasps the eschatological implications of Jesus' resurrection that it provides the solid foundation for nonviolence. The New Testament says that what happened to Jesus at his resurrection will happen to all who believe in him at his return (Romans 6:5; Philippians 3:21; 1 Corinthians 15:20-23). The New Testament also teaches that when Christ returns, he will restore all things to wholeness, even a broken creation (Romans 8:18-23; Revelation 21–22). As Paul shows at the end of his lengthy chapter on the resurrection (1 Corinthians 15), it is precisely Jesus' resurrection that is the foundation of that glorious hope. Finally, Christians refuse to kill their enemies even when that means their own death because they know where history is going. They know that the resurrected Christ will ultimately prevail.

The last verse of 1 Corinthians 15 clearly states that Christians should now begin living in the assurance of the final resurrection (15:58). N. T. Wright captures these truths wonderfully: "I know that God's new world of justice and joy, of hope for the whole earth, was launched when Jesus came out of the tomb on Easter morning, and I know that he calls his followers to live in him and by the power of his Spirit and so to be new-creation people here and now. . . . The resurrection of Jesus and the gifts of the Spirit mean that we are called to bring real and effective signs of God's renewed creation to birth even in the midst of the present age."[2]

But does that include obeying Christ's call to love our enemies rather than kill them, now in this interim time, when vicious enemies still prowl and destroy? That question leads to one of the major divides that separate Christians on the basic question of this book.

THE ALREADY/NOT YET KINGDOM

As Christian ethicist Lisa Sowle Cahill points out, one of the most important differences between Christian pacifists and Christian just war advocates is their different assessment of the implications of the fact that Christ's kingdom has already begun but is not yet complete.[3] Certainly the old age of evil and injustice remains strong. The kingdom of God is obviously not here in its fullness. That will happen only when Christ returns. And in this interim already/not yet period, just war Christians argue, Christians should sometimes use lethal force.

On the other hand, Christians who believe that Jesus' followers should never kill typically place much more emphasis on the fact that Christ's kingdom has dawned powerfully. Therefore, now, with the help of the Holy Spirit, Christians should and can live Jesus' radical kingdom ethics—including his call to love our enemies.

Is there any way to adjudicate this disagreement over the implications of the already/not yet kingdom for our topic? What in the New Testament is relevant? Several things are important.

First, despite the fact that Jesus clearly taught that the kingdom was already present but not yet here in its fullness, Jesus gives not a hint of the idea that his disciples should postpone following his teaching until the kingdom arrives in its fullness. Precisely in the passage on loving enemies, Jesus ends with the command to "be perfect, therefore, as your heavenly Father is perfect" (Matthew 5:48). A bit later he says that the person who hears his words and practices them is like the wise man who builds his house on a rock (7:24). When Jesus rejects Moses's allowance of divorce and returns to God's intention in creation, he does not say that, since the old age with its temptations is still present, divorce will sometimes still be acceptable. No. In fact, he says that if one's eyes tempt one to adultery, one should take drastic action to avoid that sin (5:29-30). Jesus does not say that sometimes because the old age continues, it will be necessary to lie. In fact, he insists that our honesty must be so genuine that we need not, should not, use oaths (5:33-37). Repeatedly, Jesus demands that his disciples must live like him (Mark 8:34; John 14:23; Matthew 28:20). There is not the slightest suggestion in Jesus that his disciples should postpone obeying his ethical teaching until the kingdom arrives in fullness.

Second, the rest of the New Testament, as we have seen, calls Christians, *even now*, to imitate Jesus' self-sacrificial love at the cross, in the church, in society, and in the economic realm (1 Peter 2:18-23; Romans 12:17-20). There is no suggestion that since injustice persists in the world, Christians should reluctantly abandon Jesus' teaching for a while.

Third, all of the New Testament insists on high ethical standards in Jesus' new messianic community.[4] The very thought that Christians might continue doing sinful things horrifies Paul (Romans 6:1-2).

The foundation of the apostle Paul's conviction that Christians live ethically faithful lives now is the fact that their faith in Christ has radically transformed them. They have been baptized into Christ's death and raised with him to a new life (Romans 6:4). Christians must not let sin reign in their lives because they have been "set free from sin" (6:12, 18). God has acted in such a way in Christ "that the righteous requirement of the law might be fully met in us, who do not live according to the flesh but according to the Spirit" (8:4). Paul tells the Corinthians that "if anyone is in Christ, the new creation has come" (2 Corinthians 5:17). Christ is the Messiah, which means that his messianic kingdom has begun. Christians are already living in the new messianic kingdom that Christ announced. Therefore they can and must live radically transformed lives.

Perhaps no biblical texts state the radical ethical transformation that genuine Christian faith produces—*now*, in this already/not yet time!—more pointedly than Ephesians 4:17 and 1 John, which is blunt: "Whoever says, 'I know him,' but does not do what he commands is a liar" (1 John 2:3-4). The writer does not suggest that Jesus' disciples should sometimes choose not to follow his commands because the world is still a wicked, vicious place.

Finally, the New Testament says that Christians should live differently from the world (John 15:18; 1 Peter 1:17-20; 2:11). Romans 12:2 specifies how Christians should live *now*: "Do not conform to the pattern of this world."

None of the texts just cited speak explicitly to the question of whether Jesus' commands may or should sometimes be temporarily suspended because the kingdom has not yet come in its fullness. And certainly none of them deal with that question with reference to Jesus' command to his disciples to love their enemies. But there is not a hint of this logic in any of what Jesus and the rest of the New Testament says. Again and again, Jesus insists that his disciples must keep his commands. Overwhelmingly, the New Testament emphasizes the radical transformation that happens to Christians with the result that they are no longer conformed to the evil practices of the world. All that evidence weighs strongly against the argument that Christians should, despite Jesus' command to love one's enemies, sometimes kill their enemies because the kingdom has not yet fully arrived.

THE IMPORTANCE OF THE CHURCH

There are many varieties of pacifism, both religious and secular. Not all emphasize the importance of community. But for the kind of biblical pacifism developed here—where Jesus' true humanity, divinity, and bodily resurrection are foundational—Jesus' new messianic community is central.

Following Jesus' radical call to love enemies is not possible for isolated individuals. Living like Jesus is finally only possible for people who repent of their sins, embrace Christ as Lord and Savior, experience the sanctifying power of the Holy Spirit, and enjoy the social support of Jesus' new kingdom community. As members of Jesus' one body, Christians hold each other accountable to live transformed lives.

When a community turns away from the sinful practices of the world and lives profoundly different lives, the response of the larger society is often hostility. A new community modeling radical love even for enemies implicitly condemns unloving behavior. And people thus rebuked (however lovingly) frequently resent persons who even indirectly point out their sin. That is why Jesus warned his followers that the world would hate them. That is why the early church understood themselves as sojourners and exiles in a foreign land. We need the strong communal support of sisters and brothers to overcome the world's hostility.

Many pacifists say that the first task of the church is to *be* the church. Some people misunderstand this statement to mean that pacifists abandon all responsibility for the larger society. Below, I will argue at length that a rejection of killing does not require abandonment of responsibility to make society more just and peaceful. What the statement rightly points to is that the first task of Christians is *now* to live the message and ethics of Jesus' new messianic kingdom. When the surrounding society says we should abandon Jesus' teaching for the sake of short-term effectiveness, we must refuse—precisely because we know that the risen Jesus is now Lord of history and that his kingdom will finally prevail. If Jesus is truly Lord and Messiah, then his way will, in the long run, also be most effective. We need the strong support of the Christian community to live now in accordance with that belief.

IS BIBLICAL NONVIOLENCE ONLY FOR SOME CHRISTIANS?

As we have just seen, truly living like Jesus is only possible for those who embrace Christ as Lord and Savior and receive the transforming power of the Holy Spirit. We should not expect that non-Christians can and will live the way Spirit-filled Christians can and should live. But that is not to say that God has two ethics: one for faithful Christians and another for others.

Historically, Christians have sometimes advocated two different ethics. Some medieval Catholics distinguished between the "counsels of perfection" (such as loving enemies), which apply only to a special class of Christians, and the normal ethical demands, which apply to everyone.

The early Anabaptist Schleitheim Confession (1527) also appears to embrace a double ethic. This confession seems to say that God does not want Christians to use the sword (which is "outside the perfection of Christ") but that God does want secular rulers to do so. Such an argument, however, is fundamentally problematic. Such a position would mean that God would never want all people in a society to become Christians because then there would be nobody to use the sword, which God desires. That position contradicts Peter's teaching that God wants "everyone to come to repentance" (2 Peter 3:9). Furthermore, to claim that God wills an ethical norm for society different from that revealed by Christ for Christians implies that there is some ethical standard that can be known outside of Christ. But if Jesus is fully human as well as fully divine, then his life and teaching provide the fundamental norm for how God desires human beings to live.

The New Testament does not say that it is God's will for the world to continue in its fallen state. Rather, the New Testament constantly invites non-Christians to embrace Christ and begin living according to Christ's kingdom norms. The fact that Jesus is both Creator of the universe as preexistent Son and Redeemer of the world as incarnate Son contradicts the idea of a dual ethic. Finally, rejecting all killing (even killing for the sake of trying to promote societal peace and justice) is God's will for all Christians, indeed all people, or it is not God's will for anyone.

Biblical pacifism rests on several central theological affirmations. If the historic creeds are correct that Jesus is true God and true man, then rejecting Jesus' teaching on loving enemies involves a fundamental Christological heresy. Only if Jesus rose bodily from the dead does it make sense to claim we should still believe that his messianic kingdom has truly begun and his followers should and can live the ethics of his dawning kingdom. The New Testament certainly does teach that Christ's kingdom is not yet here in its fullness. But nowhere does the New Testament conclude that therefore Christians should postpone living Jesus' kingdom ethics until the returning Christ brings the completion of the kingdom. On the contrary, the New Testament repeatedly insists that Christians should not be conformed to the patterns of the fallen world (Romans 12:1-2). To do that, we need the loving support of the church, Jesus' new messianic community. Lacking that communal support and the empowering presence of the Holy Spirit, non-Christians will frequently fail to live Jesus' ethic, including his call to love enemies.

QUESTIONS FOR REFLECTION AND DISCUSSION

1. Which theological issues do you think are most basic and necessary for a nonviolent stance?

2. Do most pacifists you know believe that Jesus is true God and true man? Why? Why not?

3. Do most pacifists believe that Jesus rose bodily from the dead? Why? Why not?

4. How do one's views about who Jesus is and whether he rose from the dead affect one's thinking about pacifism and nonviolence?

5. Jesus' kingdom has already begun but is not yet fully present. How is that basic to the debate between just war and pacifist Christians?

6. What points do you consider important for resolving this disagreement?

7. How is the church important for pacifist Christians? Do you think Jesus intended his call to love enemies to apply to everyone?

9

Problems with Pacifism

PACIFISTS, SOME PEOPLE charge, have no love for neighbor. They take no responsibility for history, ignoring their obligation to move society toward justice and peace. They have an unrealistic, optimistic view of human nature. In short, they are naive idealists, selfish cowards, and reprehensible free riders, benefiting from social order that they refuse to help create.

FAILING TO LOVE THE NEIGHBOR

Pacifists, it is claimed, turn their neighbor's cheek to the oppressor. They are cowards, afraid to defend a neighbor under attack. In fact, they are "free riders." They benefit from the peace and social order that others (such as the police and military) provide but make no positive contribution to that order. Pacifists let others do the dirty work.

This is clearly a serious charge. But there are significant, decisive points to make in reply. First and perhaps most important, this argument assumes that there are only two options: do nothing to defend the neighbor or use lethal weapons. Gandhi famously remarked that if those are the only two options, then of course one should kill to resist evil.

In reality, however, it is simply false to suggest that there are only two options. Always, in every situation, there is a third option: vigorous nonviolent resistance to the aggressor. As in the case of war, there is no guarantee that nonviolent resistance will succeed in the short run. But the history of the past one hundred years, and especially the past fifty, clearly demonstrates that nonviolent resistance often does succeed in defeating injustice and increasing societal wholeness. Martin Luther King Jr.'s nonviolent civil rights movement changed American history. Gandhi's nonviolent campaign for Indian independence eventually defeated the British Empire.

Nor is it the case that nonviolent resistance only works in democracies and with "humane" rulers. A massive nonviolent campaign successfully overthrew the longtime Filipino dictator Ferdinand Marcos, a result that many thought only a devastating, decade-long civil war could achieve. In 1989, Solidarity in Poland and the "revolution of the candles" in East Germany successfully used nonviolent action to bring an end to Communist dictators.

Nonviolent action works. A recent scholarly volume by Erica Chenoweth and Maria J. Stephan explored all the known cases—323 of them—of major *armed* and *unarmed* insurrections from 1900 to 2006. Their conclusion? "Nonviolent resistance campaigns were nearly twice as likely to achieve full or partial success as their violent counterparts."[1]

Furthermore, nonviolent campaigns often result in far fewer deaths. In India's nonviolent struggle for independence, only five thousand Indians died. In Algeria's violent struggle for independence, a million Algerians died. Even more staggering is the ratio. Of India's three hundred million citizens, only one in four hundred thousand died. Of Algeria's ten million citizens, one in ten was sacrificed.

Recent history demonstrates that nonviolent resistance to tyranny and injustice often succeeds. Furthermore, more and more Christians (and others) are exploring new nonviolent ways to resist evil. Major church bodies have recently called for more use of nonviolent methods. The official public policy document of the National Association of Evangelicals says: "As followers of Jesus, we should, in our civic capacity, work to reduce conflict by promoting international understanding and engaging in nonviolent conflict resolution." And a joint statement by the Vatican's Pontifical Council for Promoting Christian Unity and Mennonite World Conference sought to promote more use of nonviolence in the resolution of domestic and international disputes.

It is true that it is immoral to stand aside and do nothing when evil people oppress and destroy our neighbors, near and far. People who believe that Jesus calls them to refuse to kill *must* take the lead in developing new, better, and more vigorous forms of nonviolent resistance to evil. Unless they are ready to risk death, as soldiers do, in nonviolent campaigns against injustice and oppression, their claim to follow Jesus' way of peacemaking is a farce. But as they embrace nonviolent resistance to evil, they demonstrate that in every historical injustice, there are not just two options but three. One can do nothing, kill, or resist nonviolently. The first option is immoral. The second contradicts what Jesus taught. The third is both faithful to Jesus and, as history shows, often successful.

There is another important response to the charge that pacifists fail to love the neighbor. Too often, people making this charge forget that according to Jesus, the neighbor whom Christians must love includes the enemy. Both the evil person attacking my neighbor and the neighbor under attack are neighbors whom Jesus calls me to love.

FAILURE TO TAKE RESPONSIBILITY FOR HISTORY

In a variety of ways, many people accuse pacifists of abandoning their obligation to shape history in ways that promote peace and justice. Even prominent scholars charge that Christian pacifists abandon any attempt to control history and give the impression that they do not care about what happens in society. Daryl Charles and Timothy J. Demy claim that Anabaptist pacifists "not only abstain from political involvement and embrace nonviolence, but also abstain from all forms of civil service and most forms of public service."[2] That includes, they say, vocations like economics, social service, law, and legal theory.

It is certainly correct that faithful Christians dare not withdraw from society. Precisely because their Lord commands them to love *all* their neighbors, they must seek to promote the societal well-being of everyone. Paul insists that Christians must "do good to all people," not just Christians (Galatians 6:10). Jesus did not withdraw from society. He challenged religious leaders (Matthew 23:1-39) and political leaders (Luke 13:31-33). It was precisely his public act of nonviolent civil disobedience in overthrowing the money changers' tables in the temple that, according to Mark's gospel, moved the religious leaders to look for a way to kill him (Mark 11:15-18). Jesus ended up on the cross precisely because he challenged the societal rulers of his day.

The crucial question, however, is this: Do Jesus' kingdom teaching and ethics provide the norms for *how* one exercises social responsibility, or does one look elsewhere for those norms? If one believes what the early Christians did—that Jesus is Lord of history, that his messianic kingdom has already begun, and that Jesus' disciples are now called to live according to the norms of that dawning kingdom, which will eventually prevail throughout the universe—then faithful Christians dare not abandon Jesus' teaching in order to exercise "responsible" concern for society. They dare not, with Reinhold Niebuhr, say, "Yes Jesus, you teach unconditional love, but that does not work in the real world, so we must ignore and abandon what you taught." Faithful Christians will work for societal well-being in every way that is faithful to Jesus' teaching. But they will insist that some things they simply will not do. Human calculation of short-term effectiveness dare not overrule Jesus' ethical norms.

Nor are pacifists the only people who make this point. Just war theorists also argue that Christian morals forbid them from doing certain things even if that means military defeat. Just war theorists like Oxford professor Oliver O'Donovan insist that following just war principles means there are some things one must not do (such as intentionally targeting civilians) even if that means accepting defeat.[3] For both groups, the crucial question is not short-term effectiveness or survival, but rather what Jesus and Christian ethics demand. Obedience to Jesus' teaching must be the first ethical obligation for all Christians.

Second, of course, pacifists insist that careful analysis of effectiveness is entirely appropriate. Pacifists think about effectiveness within the larger framework of knowing that since Jesus is truly Lord of the universe, following his ethical demands will also be effective in the long run because they fit with the nature of reality. Even in the short run, as we have seen, nonviolence is often effective. Gandhi in India, King in the United States, and Walesa's Solidarity in Poland all show that nonviolence often works. Sometimes, of course, nonviolent struggles fail in the short run. But in the long run, faithfulness and effectiveness ultimately converge. Why? Precisely because Jesus is truly Lord of history. If faithfulness and effectiveness do not ultimately converge, then our Christian conviction that Jesus is truly Lord is false.

Another aspect of the charge that pacifists abandon the attempt to shape society is that they simply withdraw into their little sectarian community and ignore the larger world. It is true that sometimes pacifists have done this—often, alas, in response to severe societal persecution. But the historical record flatly contradicts any suggestion that pacifists always do this. All social scientists know that one changes society not only from the top down but from the bottom up. Simply living a wholesome family life contributes to society. So does creating new economic enterprises and educational institutions.

Mennonites have often been pointed to as examples of pacifists who neglect their obligation to shape the larger society. Yet they have contributed to social well-being in numerous ways. Mennonite Central Committee's excellent programs in relief and community development have saved and improved the lives of millions around the world. Mennonite-initiated Christian Peacemaker Teams have pioneered methods of nonviolent accompaniment in situations of violent conflict. Mennonites have pioneered Victim-Offender Reconciliation Programs, which go beyond legal procedures to bring deeper reconciliation between offender and victim. Thousands of Mennonite doctors, lawyers, educators, and agricultural specialists contribute daily to societal well-being.

Undoubtedly the most striking Anabaptist contribution to the larger society has been their pioneering of religious freedom and thus their contribution to democracy. They died by the hundreds in the sixteenth century for their insistence that the church should be able to run its own affairs free from control by the state. Slowly their demand for religious freedom prevailed, first in Holland, then in England and the new United States. Today most countries at least theoretically embrace religious freedom for all citizens.

The Anabaptists' championing of religious freedom illustrates the fact that simply creating an alternative society can have a profound political impact. Hospitals and schools for the poor emerged out of the work of the church. Slowly the larger society came to embrace healthcare and education as human rights.

The evidence is clear. Not only should Christians who oppose all killing work for the well-being of society. They do. They seek to take responsibility for history in every way that is faithful to Jesus.

IS PACIFISM BASED ON A NAIVE VIEW OF HUMAN NATURE?

Many Christians, including Reinhold Niebuhr in his famous essay "Why the Christian Church Is Not Pacifist," make this charge. Pacifists, it is alleged, ignore human sinfulness. They think people are basically good.

The first thing to say is that this claim is true of some pacifists. Niebuhr rightly criticized the theologically liberal pacifists of his day for embracing a naive, optimistic view of human nature. But the pacifism promoted in this book is based on the center of historic Christian orthodoxy, including the theological conviction that since the fall, all persons have a pervasive inclination to selfishness. Only the liberating power of the Holy Spirit can transform self-centered sinners into persons capable of truly loving their enemies. Biblical pacifism is grounded in supernatural grace, not natural human goodness.

Christians also know that they never achieve perfection in this life. But they know that they have been called and empowered to begin to live *now* the ethics of Jesus' dawning kingdom. With the apostle Paul, they know that sin still lurks within them; but as they also know, Paul never argued that because sin still lingers in the Christian, it therefore is acceptable to fornicate, lie, and steal. Why then should we argue that the persistence of sin would justify ignoring Jesus' clear call to love our enemies?

Another aspect of human sinfulness is relevant here. There is a questionable logic in the suggestion that since all persons are deeply sinful, therefore war is inevitable. Most nations, most of the time, are not at war. War happens only under certain conditions. "Slavery, dueling, lynching, vigilantism, and war are expressions of human sin under certain conditions," writes Duane K. Friesen. "If war is resorted to only under certain conditions within the international system, then we ought to determine what those conditions are and seek to create such conditions that war cannot or will not occur."[4] Conditions have changed: slavery, dueling, and lynching have largely ended. That is not to claim that people today are less sinful than persons of earlier centuries. But the form that sinfulness takes has changed. The right kind of societal changes might very well dramatically reduce the amount of warfare in the world.

Biblical pacifists love their neighbors, even engaging in daring acts of nonviolent intervention to protect their neighbors from injustice and harm. Biblical pacifists eagerly seek to move toward greater shalom, but they refuse to use methods that Jesus prohibited. And biblical pacifists take sin very seriously. Yet they also know that the transforming presence of the risen Lord in their lives enables them to love their enemies.

QUESTIONS FOR REFLECTION AND DISCUSSION

1. What are the major problems with pacifism that many critics raise? Which of these do you consider to be most substantial?

2. How would you respond to the charge that pacifists do not love their neighbors?

3. Do pacifists fail to take responsibility for promoting justice and peace?

4. How do pacifist and just war Christians agree on the question of effectiveness?

5. What are you and your congregation doing to tangibly work for peace and justice?

6. Do you agree with Niebuhr's rejection of pacifism because of its alleged naive view of human nature? How might this reality of human sinfulness support pacifism rather than the just war tradition?

10

Problems with Just War Thinking

THE JUST WAR tradition that has developed over the centuries has several key components. Just war thinkers say that certain criteria must be met before a war can be declared to be "just." First, last resort: before going to war, a nation must first explore all other reasonable alternatives. Second, just cause: the goals for which one fights must be just. Third, right attitude: the intention for fighting must be restoration of justice, not anger or retaliation. Fourth, prior declaration of war: war must first be declared by a legitimate authority. Fifth, a reasonable chance of success: if there is no reasonable chance of winning the war, one must not fight, even if one's cause is just. Sixth, noncombatant immunity: it is immoral to directly target civilians or kill prisoners of war. Seventh, proportionality: there must be a reasonable expectation that the good results of the war will exceed the horrible evils involved.

Difficult challenges have also been posed to those who embrace the just war stance. How can one kill a person and at the same time fulfill Christ's mandate to invite that person to accept Christ? How can one obey Christ's command to love one's enemies while one is killing them? Have the just war criteria been applied to real life in a way that has prevented or ended war? Since it cannot be the case that both sides in a battle are fighting a just war, why have almost no Christians not only refused to fight for their nation but instead chosen to fight on the other side when their nation fought unjustly? And since Christian just war theorists argue that Christians should refuse to fight unjust wars, why have they not established structures to help Christians make that determination? And why have they not made it a priority to demand legal protection for conscientious objectors to particular wars? What should one conclude from the fact that for centuries, just war Christians have regularly fought and killed other Christians?

Many charge that pacifists ignore the Old Testament. But do not key just war criteria (such as noncombatant immunity) also contradict clear Old Testament commands to destroy all men, women, and children? And is it really possible to predict the outcome of going to war with enough accuracy to meet the just war criterion that the good results of going to war outweigh the bad results? Finally, given the historical fact that human sinfulness and uncritical nationalism almost always lead Christians to embrace whatever war their nation declares, does the just war framework depend on a naively optimistic view of human goodness?

CAN ONE EVANGELIZE AND KILL A PERSON AT THE SAME TIME?

Jesus' last command to all his followers was to "go and make disciples of all nations" (Matthew 28:19). I do not see how it is possible to seek to kill people and at the same time be engaged in inviting them to accept Christ. One can constrain another person physically, one can boycott another person's unjust activity, one can confront another person in vigorous nonviolent action—all this and at the same time express genuine love for the person and invite them to accept the gospel. But one cannot do that as one tries to kill that person.

CAN ONE TRULY LOVE AN ENEMY AND KILL THEM AT THE SAME TIME?

Augustine of Hippo and Ambrose of Milan are the earliest Christian theologians to somewhat systematically develop the just war tradition. In the late fourth century and early fifth century, they sought to argue that it is possible to love enemies as one kills them. Augustine insists that it is an act of love to restore peace by using violence. It is even an act of love toward the aggressor. By this "kind harshness" an unjust aggressor may be helped to repent.

Yet strikingly, Augustine felt compelled to argue that Christians obeyed Christ's command to love their enemies even as they killed them *not as an outward act but as an* "inward disposition." When Jesus said turn the other cheek, Augustine claims, Jesus meant "not a bodily action, but an inward disposition."

But to restrict Jesus' call to love enemies to the inner disposition of the heart seems to ignore the context of Jesus' teaching. Jesus was rejecting the violent action of devout Jewish revolutionaries who were calling on their fellow Jews to kill the Roman imperialists. Jesus, on the other hand, was commanding his disciples to love them, even to carry their bags a second mile. That is an external act, not just an inward disposition! In fact, all Jesus' illustrations of what it means to love enemies rather than seek an "eye for an eye" involve external acts, not just inward dispositions.

HAVE THE JUST WAR CRITERIA PREVENTED OR STOPPED WARS?

The historical record demonstrates with painful clarity that the just war tradition has not been very effective in preventing unjust warfare. There are very few historical instances in which nations chose not to go to war because Christians in the government or the military argued that the proposed war did not meet the criteria of the just war tradition. Christians have, with painfully few exceptions, defended their own nation's wars. They have condemned and then accepted every new escalation of military technology. And they have developed no mechanism independent of the state to evaluate the justice of specific wars. Consistent, widespread failure of a position should raise serious questions about its usefulness.

History shows that the just war criteria are especially vulnerable to societal pressures of tribalism and jingoistic nationalism. This becomes clear when we look at the various ways just war theory has been applied in the past.

On the basis of the just war tradition, it seems that at least one side in each conflict is fighting for an unjust cause. Yet in both world wars and in the hundreds of European battles in previous centuries, Christians fought on *both* sides. If the just war tradition had functioned effectively, at least some Christians fighting on the wrong side should have realized their country's injustice and opposed the nation's military activities. In fact, the acid test of belief in the just war tradition seems to be a willingness to fight *against* one's country when it fights unjust wars. But that has hardly ever happened.

The German church's response to Hitler underlines this failure. If Allied opposition to Hitler is the classic example of a just war, then Hitler's attacks provide the classic example of unjust war. But the vast majority of German Christians, both Catholic and Protestant, supported Hitler's war.

Even in this classic illustration of an unjust war, the overwhelming majority of Christians could not faithfully apply the criteria of the just war tradition. That raises serious questions about the usefulness of the entire approach. This consistent pattern of nationalistic rationalization suggests that the hope of faithfully applying just war criteria rests on a naive view of human nature. Might consistent nonviolence be a more realistic response to this essential human sinfulness?

Throughout history the church has also denounced and then accepted each new advance in the methods of warfare. When Germany first attacked the British civilian population in aerial raids, British Christians denounced this gross immorality and vowed not to retaliate in kind. A prominent British church leader, J. H. Oldham, said in 1940: "The deliberate killing of non-combatants is murder. If war degenerates into willful slaughter of the innocent, Christians must either become pacifists or give up their religion." But three years later, he said that the distinction between aiming at military targets and aiming at civilians was not important. The government could choose whatever military necessity demanded. And Christian pilots actually participated in the Allied firebombing of German cities, including Dresden, where in one day more than a hundred thousand noncombatants perished in a huge firestorm.

The widespread failure of just war Christians to embrace and implement *selective conscientious objection* is another aspect of the weakness of that tradition. The just war tradition assumes that at least some wars declared by rulers will be unjust. In those cases, Christians who follow the just war tradition should refuse to fight. Many democracies have laws allowing conscientious objectors (those who oppose *all* war) to choose alternative service. But hardly any nation has laws recognizing *selective* conscientious objection to particular wars. And just war Christians have done very little to work for laws allowing selective conscientious objection to particular wars—even though the just war criteria, if applied with any seriousness, would require frequent conscientious objection to particular wars.

Furthermore, churches that accept the just war tradition should have organized mechanisms for assembling the insights of ethicists, theologians, social scientists, and others to examine the validity of possible wars that the nation might plausibly consider fighting. This has not happened. The isolated individual needs help to understand complex issues and withstand nationalistic propaganda. Secular governments will always rationalize current plans and narrow national self-interest. The absence of functioning mechanisms in just war churches for evaluating the validity of the wars their members may be called to fight is one measure of the failure of that tradition.

Just war ethicists argue that failure to successfully apply the just war criteria does not prove that the stance itself is wrong. But the just war tradition has been the mainstream teaching of Christian thinkers for more than fifteen hundred years. It has been the official way by which most Christian leaders have argued that faithful Christians should think about war and violence and act to avoid engagement in unjust, misguided war. Since the just war tradition has almost always failed to do that, surely that raises serious questions about whether the just war tradition is really a helpful approach.

It is technically correct that the failure of the just war tradition to prevent unjust wars does not logically prove that the stance is wrong. However, its widespread failure surely raises a serious question about its usefulness. If, when nonviolent activists sought to apply their theory to concrete situations, the result was almost always failure to reduce violence and injustice, I would agree with those who question its usefulness. The fact that history discloses very few instances where just war thinking has actually been used to avoid unjust violence surely must raise the question of whether it is a useful, effective way for the Christian church to think about war.

CHRISTIANS KILLING CHRISTIANS

With the just war tradition as their basic theoretical framework, Christians have gone to war to slaughter other Christians by the tens of thousands, hundreds of thousands, indeed millions. Before the United States entered World War I, some 46 million Protestants and 62 million Catholics were trying to kill 45 million Protestants and 63 million Catholics on the other side. In that war, Christians killed millions of other Christians. Pulpits on both sides endorsed their country's crusade.

Nor was the slaughter of Christians by Christians something new—except for the numbers killed. Catholics and Protestants fought numerous bloody battles in the almost 150 years of the wars of religion that devastated Europe after Luther sparked the Protestant Reformation.

Surely Christians killing Christians violates the New Testament teaching about the one body of Christ (Ephesians 4:1-6; Galatians 3:28). And Jesus made it clear that commitment to him was a higher allegiance even than one's commitment to mother or father (Matthew 10:37). If New Testament teaching means anything, every Christian's commitment to Christ must be a higher commitment than to one's family, political party, or nation. The little statement on a postcard circulated by Mennonite Central Committee contains a profound theological imperative: "A modest proposal for peace: Let the Christians of the world agree that they will not kill each other."

Tragically, Christians have consistently failed to do that. Again and again Christians have placed loyalty to their nation above loyalty to the one global body of Christ. As a result, Christians claiming the just war tradition as their framework have slaughtered other Christians in warfare by the millions. Surely that raises serious questions about the usefulness of the just war tradition.

THE JUST WAR TRADITION AND THE OLD TESTAMENT

In chapter 7, I wrestled with how Christians should understand all the divine commands to kill others in the Old Testament. But one other issue is important here. The just war tradition forbids what the Old Testament commands and encourages what the Old Testament condemns. The just war tradition unequivocally condemns targeting noncombatants and captured soldiers. The Old Testament repeatedly commands slaughtering all men, women, and children in a conquered territory. The just war tradition encourages preparing to defend the nation with state-of-the-art weapons. The Old Testament frequently condemns amassing and depending on military might.

Again and again, Old Testament texts command Israel to slaughter every living person in cities captured by Israel—often, the text says, at the explicit command of God. "Do not leave alive anything that breathes. Completely destroy them . . .

as the Lord your God has commanded you" (Deuteronomy 20:16-17; also, Joshua 10:28-39; 11:14-15; 1 Samuel 15:2-3). Even John Calvin acknowledged that God's command to destroy everything alive inevitably strikes us as an act of "savagery" and "a deed of atrocious and barbaric ferocity."[1] The Old Testament repeatedly tells stories about how Israel (often at the command of God) slaughtered men, women, and children after defeating their armies. On the other hand, the just war tradition explicitly forbids targeting noncombatants or killing captured enemy soldiers.

There is a second area of conflict with the just war tradition in the Old Testament. Many Old Testament texts condemn Israel for acquiring the standard military equipment of the time (especially chariots and warhorses: Deuteronomy 17:16; Psalm 20:7; 33:16-17; Hosea 10:13-14). Isaiah says: "Woe to those who go down to Egypt for help and rely on [war]horses, who trust in the multitude of their chariots and in the great strength of their horsemen, but do not look to the Holy One of Israel" (31:1).

The prophetic call to trust in Yahweh rather than state-of-the-art military equipment is certainly not the only theme in the Old Testament. But it appears with some frequency. If just war Christians followed this Old Testament summons, they would urge their nations to trust in God rather than build the strongest, best-equipped military.

It seems that the Old Testament is almost as problematic for just war Christians as for pacifists. It repeatedly commands activities that just war Christians condemn and sometimes urges an approach that they ignore. It is simply not convincing for just war Christians to claim that they are merely embracing what the Old Testament teaches about war.

IS THE JUST WAR TRADITION MORE REALISTIC ABOUT HUMAN NATURE THAN PACIFISM?

That claim is often made by just war advocates. According to their claim, pacifists assume that people are basically good. But in fact, the Christian doctrine of sin explains why people regularly do awful things to their neighbors—and why, it is claimed, just war is necessary.

Some pacifists do have a naive view of humans as basically good. But the kind of biblical pacifism advocated here fully recognizes the pervasiveness and depth of human sinfulness. Indeed, this sinful reality may explain the fact that, most of the time, selfish interests, blind tribalism, and jingoistic nationalism have prevented Christians from effectively applying the just war criteria. Instead, they have embraced virtually every war their leaders declared. Perhaps a realistic understanding of this persistent sinfulness should lead to the conclusion that a pacifist stance fits better with our sinful nature than a just war stance. Pacifists know—before their nation makes powerful emotional appeals to fight a war—that Jesus calls his followers always to refuse to kill. That belief protects against the ongoing temptation of quickly yielding to emotional appeals to narrow self-interest and excessive nationalism better than if one thinks one should carefully and thoughtfully apply the just war criteria. Given the reality of human sinfulness, the pacifist position is probably more realistic than the just war stance.

The cumulative effect of the problems with the just war tradition lead to serious doubt about the usefulness of that tradition. One cannot invite someone to accept the gospel and simultaneously kill that person. It is very doubtful that one can implement Jesus' command to love one's enemies and kill them at the same time. There is little evidence to show that the just war tradition has prevented war. Nor has it encouraged significant numbers of just war Christians to refuse to fight their nation's unjust wars. The scandal of Christians killing Christians by the thousands and millions in their nation's wars underlines the fact that Christians repeatedly fail to act on the implications of the just war tradition. At least for anyone who seeks to justify participation in war on the basis of the Old Testament, it is problematic that the just war tradition forbids what the Old Testament frequently commands and encourages what the Old Testament condemns.

In light of these failures and problems, it is highly plausible to argue that pacifism fits better with the Christian understanding of the prevalence of sin than does the just war tradition.

QUESTIONS FOR REFLECTION AND DISCUSSION

1. Which of the stated problems for the just war tradition do you consider most convincing? Least convincing? Why? What other problems would you add?

2. Which of the arguments in this chapter would just war Christians find most convincing? How do you think they would argue against the viewpoint argued in this chapter?

3. Do you have Christian friends in the just war tradition (if you are a pacifist) or in the pacifist tradition (if you are a just war Christian)? If not, why not? What could you do to get to know people who hold a different viewpoint than you do?

4. How might a just war congregation and a pacifist congregation develop a Christian dialogue on this issue?

11

What If Most (or All) Christians Became Pacifists?

BOTH REPEATED HEADLINES and careful scholars remind us that powerful terrorist groups seek to destroy the United States, Israel, and "Western values." Radical Islamic terrorists are only a small part of the global Muslim community. But they have sometimes terrorized, raped, beheaded, and slaughtered Christians in the last couple of decades. Groups like ISIS and Al Qaeda are a genuine threat to many people, especially Christians. Like vicious people of the past—Hitler, Stalin, Pol Pot—they seem to respond to nothing except force. The only way to stop their vicious behavior seems to be to fight and kill them.

If most or all Christians became pacifists, would evil not rage unchecked? Would not Hitler's racist Nazism, Stalin's totalitarian communism, or Osama bin Laden's ruthless terrorism conquer the world?

ORIGEN TO CELSUS

A very similar question faced the early church. Sometime about AD 180, a fairly well-informed Roman pagan named Celsus wrote a sharp attack on Christians. One of his central arguments was that since Christians refuse to kill, if all Romans became Christians, barbarians would invade and destroy the Roman Empire.

More than fifty years after Celsus's attack, Origen (perhaps the most widely read Christian author in the first half of the third century) wrote a reply. Origen agreed with Celsus that Christians refuse to kill. But he insisted that if all Romans became Christians, God would protect them. Origen acknowledged that sometimes God does allow evil people to kill Christians. But persecution lasts only as long as God allows it. And despite frequent persecution in the second and third centuries, Christianity actually flourished and expanded rapidly.

I think that the first and most important response to the concern of this chapter is essentially the reply of Origen. Christians believe that the risen Lord Jesus is now "ruler of the kings of the earth" (Revelation 1:5). We know that "all authority in heaven *and on earth* has been given" to him (Matthew 28:18, emphasis added). Jesus told Pilate, "You would have no power over me if it were not given to you from above" (John 19:11). Sometimes God allows Christians to suffer martyrdom. Sometimes God marvelously, even miraculously, prevents that. But we know that the "gates of hell shall not prevail against it [the church]" (Matthew 16:18 KJV).

We know where history is going. We know the final outcome. We know that in God's time, Christ will return and complete the victory over all evil. Until then, Christ's faithful followers will sometimes experience terrible persecution. But they cannot be defeated. And the risen One, who is *now* Lord of heaven and earth, has promised: "I am with you always, to the very end of the age" (Matthew 28:20). As the evidence of the early church demonstrates, the witness of faithful martyrs trusting the Lord even in death draws more and more people to become disciples.

NONVIOLENT CHALLENGE AND DIALOGUE

Yet the answer of Origen is not the only important thing to say. For one thing, Christians who believe Christ calls them never to kill must not become passive in the face of evil and injustice. There is a vast range of powerful ways to work nonviolently against injustice. Especially in the past hundred years, courageous leaders like Gandhi and Martin Luther King Jr. have demonstrated that nonviolent action can be an effective way to challenge and overcome evil. As we have seen, daring Christian leaders in the Philippines, Poland, East Germany, and Liberia led the way in successful nonviolent campaigns that succeeded in overthrowing vicious dictators.[1] If most Christians became pacifists, they would invest large resources in preparing for and engaging in nonviolent campaigns against injustice and violence.

Second, pacifist Christians have a great deal to contribute to resolving the current conflicted relationship between the world's two largest religions, Christianity and Islam. Only a small number of Muslims are terrorists. But the larger Muslim world has genuine grievances against Christians. Many Muslims still reference the medieval Crusades, when European Christians invaded the Holy Land, controlled for centuries by Muslim rulers, and slaughtered tens of thousands of Muslims. In the nineteenth century, white "Christian" European colonial powers used their military superiority to dominate Muslim societies from North Africa to Indonesia. With partial justification, many Muslims blame their poverty and other problems on "Christian" nations.

I do not believe that the "Christian" West is to blame for all or most of the problems—poverty, lack of modern education, dictatorial regimes—in many majority Muslim nations. But we have contributed to the problem. And that fact gives some credibility to the Islamic terrorists' claim that the only solution is to seek and destroy the "Christian" West.

Almost every informed Western leader knows that Islamic terrorism cannot be defeated only with arms. The primary struggle is in the realm of ideas. We must help youth tempted by violence to see that freedom, economic development, scientific advance, and peaceful cooperation are the way forward.

PEACEMAKING ACTIVITIES

In the early 1990s, a group of pacifist and just war Christian ethicists began a dialogue that has led to what is called "just peacemaking." Without resolving their essential disagreement about whether Christians should ever kill, they agree that there are many effective nonviolent practices that promote peace: fostering sustainable economic development, advancing democracy and human rights, and so on.

Both just war and pacifist Christians can and should work together on nonviolent, just peacemaking. Pacifists, however, should be especially active. And they are. Mennonite Central Committee, a worldwide ministry of Anabaptist churches, invests tens of millions of dollars every year in economic development—including work in impoverished Muslim nations—and has been active in assisting Syrian refugees from the prolonged war in Syria. Christian Peacemaker Teams (which grew out of

Mennonite circles) has been active in Israel-Palestine, using the tactics of nonviolent intervention, seeking to promote peace with justice for both Israelis and Palestinians.

Christian pacifists are not closely identified with the military activities of Western nations in Muslim countries. Precisely for that reason, they have a unique opportunity to initiate dialogue and cooperative programs of social, educational, and economic development with Muslims who are deeply suspicious of Western initiatives. They can begin conversations and programs that would be considered highly suspect and probably rejected if proposed by official representatives of Western nations. Pacifists have a unique opportunity to lead the way toward greatly reducing one of today's most serious conflicts—one which, if unresolved, could lead to an incredibly destructive "conflict of civilizations."

Muslim-Christian conflict, of course, is not the only area of violence in our world. Selfish and violent persons threaten the property and lives of people in every society. Police help prevent societies from slipping into anarchy. And aggressive nations frequently threaten their neighbors.

For Christians who believe our Lord calls us never to kill, a serious discussion of how we should deal with the issues of police and national defense would require at least two other books. Here, in a very few paragraphs, I can only hint at what could be developed at much greater length.

People disagree about whether it would be possible someday to move to completely nonviolent police work. But it is clearly the case that the criminal justice system, including the work of police, could be greatly improved through new approaches of restorative justice and nonviolent policing.

Pacifists have pioneered the now widely influential Victim-Offender Reconciliation Programs, now often called

Victim-Offender Dialogue or Victim-Offender Conferencing. These programs help offenders accept responsibility for their actions, face the people they have harmed, and seek to repair the damage they have caused. A vast number of such programs now exist. Extensive research has shown that these programs reduce recidivism, improve the lives of both victims and offenders, and reduce the cost of criminal justice.

Other nonlethal approaches are being tested. An increasing number of police departments use electroshock weapons, which can incapacitate but do not kill. The use of this type of weapon and pepper spray could be greatly expanded. In recent decades community policing—an approach that uses more foot patrols and focuses on building trust and relationships with citizens in their neighborhoods—has been embraced in a number of communities. If combined with efforts to reduce structural factors nurturing crime (such as racism and lack of economic opportunity), much greater adoption of the best community policing efforts would reduce crime in a largely nonviolent way.

Citizen patrols, in which unarmed local residents volunteer to walk at night to discourage crime, have occurred for decades in some neighborhoods. Christian Peacemaker Teams has modeled a version of this in Cleveland. Pacifists should greatly expand this effort, training large numbers of church members to patrol their neighborhoods and embrace other nonviolent responses to crime.

Pacifists can now act in many ways to develop and encourage more widespread use of nonviolent methods in policing.

CIVILIAN-BASED DEFENSE

Gene Sharp is the most distinguished advocate of civilian-based defense (CBD). CBD is a national policy in which the entire population of a country is trained to oppose invaders with non-violent noncooperation. Michael Walzer, in his book *Just and Unjust Wars*, devotes several pages to Sharp's proposal of CBD. Walzer notes that there is no evidence that it works, since no nation has ever fully tried it. And Walzer believes that it would only work against an invader who embraced fundamental moral values.

Actually, there is evidence that something like CBD partially worked against Hitler. After Hitler invaded, both Norway and Denmark engaged in widespread national nonviolent resistance and civil disobedience. Using nonviolent techniques, Norway saved half of the country's Jews and Denmark saved 93 percent of the Danish Jews.

Military specialists have urged more intensive study of CBD. When Gene Sharp's book *The Politics of Nonviolent Action* appeared, with its many examples of nonmilitary defense, U.S. military journals of the army, navy, and air force reviewed it positively and recommended that readers give it "serious consideration."

In their famous 1983 pastoral letter, *The Challenge of Peace*, U.S. Catholic bishops cited the work of Gene Sharp and urged further study of CBD. They acknowledge that CBD would be costly. But they urge us to compare those costs with the almost certain devastation of a major war.

What would happen if all the Christians in the United States (or the whole world) would decide that Jesus calls us to refuse to kill? We would suffer greatly. Evil people would kill many millions. We would suffer a huge loss of possessions. The suffering would be immense. But using the methods of war has also been deadly. Eighty-six million people died in wars just between 1900 and 1989. War also has enormous costs.

If all Christians decided to love their enemies rather than try to kill them, I think it is reasonable to expect that fewer people would die from violence in the next hundred years than in the past century. And sometimes nonviolent resistance would be stunningly successful.

There is clear evidence from successful nonviolent campaigns that courageous nonviolent resistance sometimes moves the hearts of hardened soldiers. When a million Filipino citizens dared to stand in front of the tanks sent by the ruthless dictator President Marcos to crush them, the soldiers hesitated. One eyewitness reported: "The soldiers atop the armored carriers pointed their guns of every make at the crowd, but their faces portrayed agony. . . . The soldiers did not have the heart to pull the triggers on civilians armed only with their convictions."[2] Praying nuns and unarmed civilians conquered a vicious dictator.

Not always, of course. There would be terrible suffering and many deaths—probably millions. But would there be as many as in the wars of the twentieth century? And what would Christ our Lord do if his disciples all chose to face death rather than kill their enemies? Again, we cannot know in advance.

WHAT IF . . . ?

I expect that if most Christians today would decide to love their enemies rather than try to fight them with violence, we would experience perhaps the most amazing epoch of church history. Millions of Christians would suffer and die. But millions of astonished observers would decide to embrace Christ. I even dare to expect that fewer people would die than if we continue on the path of violent defense, developing ever more lethal weapons. That expectation, of course, is only a hope. Since the fourth century, most Christians have chosen war rather than nonviolence. We will have empirical evidence of my hopeful expectation only if most Christians dare to act on the conviction that their Lord summons them to love their enemies rather than kill them.

QUESTIONS FOR REFLECTION AND DISCUSSION

1. What would most of your friends think about the issue posed by this chapter?

2. What do you think of the response to the question by Origen, the early Christian writer?

3. What would Christians do if large numbers *did* forsake all killing?

4. How successful do you think Christian pacifists would be in dealing with people committed to violent approaches to conflict?

5. How much police work do you think could be done non-violently? Why is not more done in this way?

6. Do you think civilian-based national defense needs discussion? Why? How could that discussion be encouraged?

7. What do you think would happen if all Christians rejected all killing?

8. What do *you* feel led to do about the topic of this chapter? What might your church do?

12

Nonviolence and the Atonement

THE FOUNDATION OF Christian nonviolence lies not in some calculation of effectiveness. It rests in the cross. The ultimate ground of the biblical summons to love enemies is the nature of God revealed first in Jesus' teaching and life and then most powerfully in his death and resurrection.

Jesus did not say that one should practice loving nonviolence because it would always transform vicious enemies into bosom friends. The cross stands as a harsh reminder that love for enemies does not always work—at least not in the short run. Jesus grounded his call to love enemies in the very nature of God: "Love your enemies and pray for those who persecute you, *that* you may be children of your Father in heaven" (Matthew 5:44-45, emphasis added; compare 5:9). God loves God's enemies. Instead of promptly destroying sinners, God continues to shower the good gifts of creation upon them. Since that is the way God acts, those who want to be God's sons and daughters must do likewise.

Earlier we discussed both Jesus' unconventional teaching on God's prodigal forgiveness and also his unorthodox view of a suffering Messiah. The link between these central affirmations of Jesus and his teaching on nonviolence now becomes clearer. Jesus' conception of the suffering Messiah who goes to the cross as a ransom for sinners underlines most powerfully his teaching on God's way of dealing with enemies. At the Last Supper, Jesus stated unequivocally that he was going to die for the sake of others. "This is my blood of the covenant, which is poured out for many for the forgiveness of sins" (Matthew 26:28).

The cross is the ultimate demonstration that God deals with God's enemies through suffering love. This receives its clearest theological expression in Paul: "God demonstrates his own love for us in this: While we were still sinners, Christ died for us. . . . While we were God's *enemies*, we were reconciled to him through the death of his Son" (Romans 5:8, 10, emphasis added). Jesus' vicarious cross for sinners is the foundation and deepest expression of Jesus' command to love one's enemies. As the substitutionary view of the atonement indicates, we are enemies in the double sense that sinful persons are hostile to God and that the just, holy Creator hates sin (Romans 1:18). On the cross the One who knew no sin was made sin for us sinful enemies (2 Corinthians 5:21; Galatians 3:10-14).

CHALLENGES TO TRADITIONAL UNDERSTANDINGS OF THE ATONEMENT

This idea plunges one into the midst of intense modern debate about the nature of the atonement. Is the violence of the cross inconsistent with Jesus' teaching on nonviolence? Is the cross divine child abuse? Have we misunderstood Paul's conception of sin? As a result, is the idea that Jesus' death paid the penalty for our sins a mistake? Is the widespread evangelical idea of substitutionary atonement—that is, that Jesus took our sins upon himself, becoming our substitute so that we might receive salvation—really what the New Testament says? And if Jesus' substitutionary death on the cross is the primary purpose of Jesus' coming to earth (as some evangelicals claim), is there any connection between the atonement and Christian ethics? Let's consider some of these questions.

J. DENNY WEAVER

Theologian J. Denny Weaver argues that Jesus' death "accomplishes nothing for the salvation of sinners." Weaver insists that Jesus did not come to die and God did not will Jesus' death on the cross. "Satisfaction atonement *in any form* depends on divinely sanctioned violence," he writes.[1] Such a view, Weaver claims, makes God the author of Jesus' death, which is divine child abuse. It is a picture, Sharon Baker claims, of "a cruel father who demands the blood of an innocent person."[2]

Furthermore, it nurtures unhealthy attitudes among Christians, encouraging women to accept abuse and minorities to accept domination. Finally, it involves a heretical doctrine of the Trinity.[3]

I find Weaver's views fundamentally unbiblical at many points. He simply ignores large parts of the New Testament. Jesus said he came "to give his life as a ransom for many" (Mark 10:45). The Gospels, Acts, and the Epistles all say that Jesus' death on the cross was according to the eternal will of God (for example, Acts 2:23).

The claim that Jesus' death has no significance for our salvation contradicts numerous New Testament statements. Paul regularly argues that we are reconciled to God by the death of Christ (Romans 3:21-25; 5:9-10; Galatians 3:13-14).

What about divine child abuse? If we see an angry God bludgeoning the innocent man Jesus, then this surely is divine child abuse. But that ignores the fact that the Trinity is present at the cross. The Father and the Spirit suffer the agony of the cross every bit as much as the Son. The Trinity wills the cross.

What about the argument that we are involved in logical contradiction and a heretical doctrine of the Trinity if we say both that Jesus taught nonviolence and God willed Jesus' death? This would be a logical contradiction only if Jesus condemns violence in precisely the same way that God uses violence at the cross. But that is not the case. The action of an infinite God substituting Godself for sinful persons at the cross is not identical with the action of finite persons using violence against other persons.

It is very important to note that Jesus did not see any contradiction here. Jesus clearly said his followers should love their enemies, thus being children of the heavenly Father (Matthew 5:43-48). But the same Jesus talked about God's wrath against sinners, divine punishment of evildoers, and eternal separation from God (Matthew 25:41-46). *Jesus* does not find these two ideas to be contradictory.

Nor does the rest of the New Testament. As we will see below, the teaching that God is angry at and punishes sin appears throughout the New Testament—right alongside the most amazing statements about God's overflowing love. We ought to submit to what Jesus and the New Testament tell us about God punishing sinners and the Son taking our place at the cross rather than reject (on the basis of some alleged logical contradiction) one part of what Jesus and the New Testament teach.

It is also important to remember that the Bible calls on believers to imitate God at some points and not at others. Finite human beings are radically different from God. We do not create out of nothing. Our understanding of how holiness and love, justice and mercy, fit together in perfect harmony is dreadfully incomplete.

One of the places where the New Testament *specifically* forbids persons from imitating God is just at this point. God, the New Testament teaches more than once, does rightly execute vengeance on evildoers. But the New Testament explicitly says that Christians should *not* do that (Romans 12:19; Hebrews 10:30; 1 Peter 2:23). Finite human beings simply do not know enough to rightly combine holiness and love in a way that punishes evil the way God justly does. Yet that does not mean that God should not. Nor does it mean there is a contradiction in the Trinity or in Jesus' own teaching when the incarnate One tells us that the trinitarian God loves God's enemies and also punishes sinners. Only an infinite, all-knowing, all-loving, and holy God knows how holiness and love fit together perfectly in the very being of God.

One final point: Weaver and others, such as Joanne Carlson Brown and Rebecca Parker, seem to think that the satisfaction view of the atonement encourages women to submit passively to abuse and the oppressed to passively accept oppression.[4] But that is to claim too much. One can and should agree that an understanding of the atonement that focuses *exclusively* on Christ as our substitute on the cross so that we can be forgiven by a holy God does cut the link with ethics. It does make it easy for white racists and male chauvinists to continue in their sin. It does run the danger of nurturing passivity in the face of abuse and oppression. But none of those problems follow

if one has a fully biblical understanding of the cross and salvation. Christ not only came to die as a substitute for us. He
also came to bring the inbreaking reign of God; to combat and
break the power of evil, including sexism and racism; to transform and empower us so that believers now can live according
to the norms of Christ's dawning kingdom and join Christ in
the battle against all that enslaves, abuses, and destroys people.

The solution to the inadequacies of an *exclusively* substitutionary view of the atonement is not to throw away what that
view rightly teaches. It is rather to see that metaphor in the
much larger context of everything the New Testament teaches
about the atonement. It is also to place all of that within Jesus'
proclamation that the messianic kingdom has begun and his
disciples can and should even now live the life of that new kingdom. The goal of the atonement is not only forgiveness of sins
but also freedom from the power of sin so we can now live the
kingdom life that Jesus taught.

C. H. DODD, "SINS," AND SIN

Many scholars have argued that, for Paul, God's wrath is not
divine anger at sins committed but rather an "inevitable process
of cause and effect in a moral universe."[5] What the cross needs
to accomplish, therefore, is not forgiveness of *sins* but liberation,
deliverance, from the enslaving power of *Sin*. Consequently, the
atonement involves Christ conquering evil, not Christ offering himself as a substitute for our sins. This view of the atonement—that Jesus liberates from evil—is called *Christus Victor*.

That the New Testament does sometimes talk of Christ's
atoning work in this way is clear (as in 1 John 3:8; Hebrews
2:14-15).[6] But an *exclusive* emphasis on this understanding of
the atonement ignores other clear texts that speak of "sins" in

the plural and say that Christ became our substitute to offer sinners forgiveness for our *sins*. And Christ's substitutionary death happened because God, who is both holiness and love and hates and punishes sins, freely chose out of unfathomable love to accomplish our forgiveness that way.

Frequently Paul talks about sins in the plural (Romans 4:7; 11:27; 1 Corinthians 15:3). Furthermore, Paul quite clearly says that Jesus became a substitute and a curse for us, taking the guilt for our sins upon himself (Romans 5:6-11; 2 Corinthians 5:21; Galatians 3:10-13).

The result? God no longer reckons or imputes our sins to us (2 Corinthians 5:19). When we trust not in our good deeds but in God, "who justifies the ungodly," our faith is credited as justification (Romans 4:4-6). And Paul goes on to explain what that justification means by quoting Psalm 32:1-2, which says that someone is blessed whose sins are forgiven rather than being counted against such a person (Romans 4:7-8). And, as Paul has explained a bit earlier, that justification comes through faith in Jesus' death on the cross (3:21-26).

GOD'S WRATH

Does Jesus' cross deal with God's wrath? Does God's wrath require Jesus' death so that God may forgive sinful enemies? And if so, does that contradict Jesus' teaching that God loves his enemies?

Many modern people want to dismiss the idea of God's wrath and speak only of God's love. But the New Testament speaks of God's wrath at least thirty times (as in Romans 1:18; 2:1-8; 3:5). But does that mean God is angry at sinners?

C. H. Dodd and others, as reported above, have argued that God's wrath is an impersonal process of cause and effect built into the structure of the universe. As Paul says in Romans 1, God gives sinners over to the natural destructive consequences of their evil acts (1:24, 26, 28). The fact that sinful actions produce destructive results does not mean, it is said, that God is angry at sinners. God is only angry at sin.

It is true that sometimes the object of God's wrath is sin itself (as in Romans 1:18). But in other passages, the object of God's wrath is evildoers (Luke 21:23; John 3:36; Romans 2:5; 1 Thessalonians 2:16). Sin, as David recognized so clearly in confessing his adultery, is first of all an offense against God (Psalm 51:4). After listing a number of sins, Ephesians 5:6 says: "Because of such things God's wrath comes on those who are disobedient."

Repeatedly the Bible says that death is a central aspect of the punishment of sin. "The wages of sin is death" (Romans 6:23). But Christ has taken the curse of sin upon himself, dying as our substitute so that those who have faith in Christ are now justi-fied, forgiven, and thus free from God's wrath against sinners.

But does this mean that God could not have forgiven us unless Christ had died as our substitute? Some evangelicals say that. They say that God *could not* have forgiven us if Christ had not died for us.

I believe the New Testament clearly says that God *did* accom-plish our justification through Christ's substitutionary death on the cross. But I know of no biblical passage claiming that was the *only* way our holy God could forgive us. That the trinitar-ian God chose to substitute Godself in a most astounding way underlines that God is both love and holiness. It demonstrates more clearly than anything I can imagine that sin is a terrible re-ality that our holy God refuses to ignore. But the crucifixion of God incarnate does not mean that was the only way God could forgive us. It simply reveals in a most amazing way that God is both holiness and love. An infinite, all-knowing, all-loving God could have chosen any number of ways to forgive us.

But does not Hebrews 9:22 say that "without the shedding of blood there is no forgiveness"? Some think this verse means that God could not forgive our sins unless Jesus died for us. To interpret the statement in that way, however, ignores the first part of the verse: "The *law* requires that *nearly everything* be cleansed with blood, and without the shedding of blood there is no forgiveness" (emphasis added). The text is talking about the situation in the Old Testament. And even then, the text says, there were exceptions.

It is striking that on Israel's annual day of atonement, when the high priest made atonement for all the sins of the Israelites, the goat bearing those sins was not even killed (Leviticus 16:21-22)! Jesus repeatedly declared—on his own authority and without any requirement that sacrifice must be offered at the temple—that people's sins are forgiven (Mark 2:1-12). Clearly, both testaments teach us that God normally uses sacrifices (animals in the Old Testament, Jesus' death in the New Testament) as God forgives sins, yet also that God sometimes forgives sins without any blood sacrifice.

The fact that God chose to accomplish our forgiveness through the incarnate Son's death on the cross reveals most vividly that God is both love and holiness. But that does not mean God's wrath against sin and sinners is equal to God's love for everyone. God is love in a way that God is not wrath.

Exodus 20:5-6 declares that whereas God's punishment for sin lasts only briefly, God's steadfast love (*hesed*) endures for a thousand generations! Again and again and again, various psalms declare that God's "love endures forever" (Psalms 106:1;

107:1; 118:1-4). God's "anger lasts only a moment, but his favor lasts a lifetime" (30:5).

The Trinity is love from all eternity. Before creation, God had no wrath. God's holy wrath follows human sin. In fact, it is God's love that prompts God's anger at sinners. Precisely because God loves all people with unfathomable love, God is angry when people harm and destroy themselves and others. Mary Schertz rightly says that "the wrath of God is the truth-telling force of God's love."[7] And God's love continues even as God punishes (Jeremiah 9:7-10). Nowhere is God's love more powerfully revealed than at the cross, where the Trinity somehow experiences crucifixion as the eternal Son becomes a curse for us and dies for our sins.

If crucifixion were the end of the story, then we would need to conclude that God's wrath is at least equal to God's love. But the story continues on Easter morning. The resurrection loudly declares that God's love for sinful enemies far outweighs God's wrath against sinners. The resurrection of the one who died for our sins proves that Jesus was right in teaching that God is like the father of the prodigal son. God stands with arms stretched wide open, eager to forgive our sins and welcome us back as forgiven sons and daughters.

MULTIPLE METAPHORS OF THE ATONEMENT

I agree with the many theologians and biblical scholars who find all the biblical metaphors of the atonement complementary and important.[8] Rejecting any one metaphor involves ignoring or denying a significant part of what the New Testament says about the atonement. It is also, as I have said earlier, absolutely essential to understand the atonement within the context of Jesus' gospel of the kingdom.

THE MORAL METAPHOR

In this metaphor, Jesus' basic role is that of teacher and example, because one fundamental human problem is ignorance. This model is obviously rooted in key New Testament teachings (such as 1 John 3:16). This model focuses well the ethical demands of Christian faith, including love for enemies.

By itself, however, this metaphor of the atonement is inadequate. Unfortunately, evil in the world lies much deeper than mere ignorance. It rests in radically self-centered persons and demonic forces and the social structures they have helped to distort. We need a powerful Savior who can conquer the forces that enslave us.

THE SUBSTITUTIONARY METAPHOR

In this model Jesus' role is that of substitute, because one fundamental aspect of our problem is that sinners stand condemned as guilty before a holy God. As we have seen, a great deal of biblical material contains this metaphor (as in 2 Corinthians 5:21).

Taken *by itself,* however, the substitutionary metaphor of the atonement is also inadequate. By itself, the substitutionary view largely ignores Christ's teaching and proclamation of the kingdom and his victory over the forces of evil during his life and at Easter. If one reduces the atonement merely to Jesus' death for our sins, one abandons the New Testament understanding of the gospel of the kingdom and severs the connection between the cross and ethics. Understood that way, the cross seems totally disconnected from Jesus' summons to love our enemies.

THE CHRISTUS VICTOR METAPHOR

In this view of the atonement, Jesus' primary role is as conqueror of evil, because one fundamental part of our problem is the power of evil, whether seen in self-centered persons, demonic beings, corrupt social structures, or death itself. Again, this metaphor is rooted solidly in the New Testament (as in 1 John 3:8; 2:14). The *Christus Victor* motif moves beyond an exclusively individualistic understanding of sin and salvation and points to the social and cosmic aspects of salvation.

Taken *by itself*, however, this view too is inadequate. Because this model points to the evil forces *outside* the individual, it is easy for proponents of this view to underemphasize the personal side of sin, guilt, and responsibility.

COMPLEMENTARY METAPHORS

Some people think that these different metaphors of the atonement are incompatible. But I see no need whatsoever to reject one biblical metaphor in order to affirm another. It is only when we take one view and emphasize it in a one-sided or exclusive way that we have problems. Rather, we need to see how the three views complement each other. And placing them in the context of the gospel of the kingdom helps us understand Jesus' interrelated roles as teacher, victor, and substitute.

As messianic proclaimer of the kingdom of God, Jesus taught a radical ethic of love (the moral metaphor). From his Sermon on the Mount through his death on the cross, he taught and modeled the way of love, even for enemies. Living his costly ethics, however, is possible only for forgiven sinners who are empowered by the Spirit.

As nonviolent messianic conqueror, Jesus inaugurated the kingdom, battling with Satan and all the forces of evil (the *Christus Victor* metaphor). He conquered diseases and demons in his public ministry. On the cross, he broke the power of Satan, and on Easter morning he arose triumphant over death itself, enabling his disciples, in the power of the Spirit, to live Jesus' kingdom ethics now.

As Isaiah's suffering servant, Jesus died on the cross as our substitute (the substitutionary metaphor). As a result, we can stand before our holy God despite our sins.

Understanding the atonement in the context of Jesus' gospel of the kingdom underlines the community-building aspect of Jesus' saving work. Jesus not only preached the gospel of the kingdom; he also formed a new kingdom community of women and men, prostitutes and royal servants, tax collectors and respectable folk. A reconciled community is central to God's plan of salvation (Titus 2:14). Scot McKnight is right: the "atonement is all about creating a society in which God's will is actualized—on planet earth, in the here and now."[9] And that includes loving our enemies.

That God incarnate died for sinful enemies is the deepest foundation for Jesus' call to love our enemies. Rather than being a problem for a nonviolent Christian ethic, the atonement provides the most solid foundation. The cross is not an angry God bludgeoning an innocent man. It is the three persons of the Trinity together embracing the agony of Roman crucifixion to accomplish our salvation. That the Trinity chose such awful reality to accomplish our forgiveness demonstrates with unspeakable clarity that God is both holy and loving. But the fact that God substitutes Godself for us at the cross demonstrates that God's wrath is but for a moment and God's love is everlasting.

If one claims that the substitutionary view of the atonement is the *only* important view, then one truly cuts the link between the atonement and ethics. But that is a one-sided, unbiblical position. It ignores the clear New Testament teaching on the moral and *Christus Victor* metaphors of the atonement. And it fails to place the cross in the context of Jesus' gospel of the kingdom. At the heart of Jesus' gospel is the teaching that the members of Jesus' dawning kingdom should love their enemies. And the fact that the Trinity somehow embraces Roman crucifixion, dying for sinful enemies, is is the deepest foundation for that teaching.

It is a tragedy of our time that many of those who appropriate the biblical understanding of Christ's vicarious cross fail to see its direct implications for the problem of war and violence. And it is equally tragic that some of those who emphasize pacifism and nonviolence fail to ground it in Christ's atonement. Since Jesus commanded his followers to love their enemies and then died as the incarnate Son to demonstrate that God reconciles God's enemies by suffering love, any rejection of the nonviolent way in human relations seems to me to involve an inadequate doctrine of the atonement. If God in Christ has reconciled God's enemies by God's suffering servanthood, should not those who want to follow Christ also treat their enemies in the same way?

QUESTIONS FOR REFLECTION AND DISCUSSION

1. What is the connection between nonviolence and the atonement? Why is this important?

2. What problems or conflicts with nonviolence do some people find in the metaphors of the atonement?

3. How decisive do you think Weaver's objections are? Why?

4. What is Dodd's view? How does it affect one's understanding of the atonement? How do you evaluate it?

5. Is it important to speak of God's wrath against sin and sinners? Why?

6. How do you evaluate the claim that the only way God could forgive us was for Jesus to die as our substitute?

7. Are God's love and God's wrath equal? Why?

8. What is the inadequacy of each metaphor of the atonement if taken alone?

9. Do you think it is important to place the metaphors of the atonement within Jesus' gospel of the kingdom? Why or why not?

13

Christians and Killing in Church History

WHAT CAN WE learn about our topic from the history of the church? From the early church, before Emperor Constantine in AD 313 decreed the end of persecution of Christians? From the time, post-Constantine, when the Roman emperors favored Christians? From the small but growing number of Christian pacifists from the sixteenth through the nineteenth centuries? From the large number of new denominations in the past century that were originally pacifist? And from the recent official support for pacifism in the Catholic church?

PRE-CONSTANTINIAN CHRISTIANITY

Scholars have offered contradictory views about Christians' thinking and practice about killing in the centuries between the end of the New Testament and the decree of Constantine in AD 313. Some modern scholars have claimed that the early church was essentially pacifist. Others have argued that the thinking of the early church on killing (especially in warfare) was "small, divided and ambiguous."[1]

There have been hundreds of books and articles on the early church's views on killing. But no one had ever collected in one volume all relevant sources (literary and archeological). I did that in my book *The Early Church on Killing.*[2] It is now possible to say with some precision what the Christians before Constantine said and did.

There is not a single extant Christian author before Constantine who says killing or joining the military by Christians is ever legitimate. Whenever our extant texts mention killing—whether in abortion, capital punishment, or war—they always say Christians must not do that. There are a substantial number of passages written over two centuries on this topic. Every Christian statement on killing and war up until the time of Constantine to which we have access says Christians must not kill, even in war.

No early Christian writer stated the absolute prohibition of all killing more firmly than Lactantius (AD 250–325). At the court of the Emperor Diocletian during widespread persecution of Christians, Lactantius wrote *The Divine Institutes*, a brilliant defense of Christian faith in superb Ciceronian Latin. He condemned every kind of killing: abortion, infanticide, capital punishment, gladiatorial contests, war.

> For when God forbids us to kill, he not only prohibits us from open violence, which is not even allowed by the public laws, but he warns us against the commission of those things which are esteemed lawful among people. Thus it will be neither lawful for a just man [a Christian] to engage in military service . . . nor to accuse anyone of a capital charge because

it makes no difference whether you put a person to death by word or rather by sword, since it's the act of putting to death itself which is prohibited. Therefore with regard to this precept of God, there ought to be no exception at all but that it is always unlawful to put to death a person, whom God willed to be a sacred creature.[3]

It is also true that in the late second century, and then increasingly in the later third century and the first decade of the fourth century, there is evidence (both in Christian writings and in archeological data) that some Christians were serving in the Roman army—at least a few by 173 and a substantial number by the late third and early fourth centuries. Unfortunately, our sources do not enable us to say how many.

Apparently in the later third and early fourth centuries, an increasing number of the Christian laity did not live what their Christian leaders taught. That disconnect—between teaching or preaching and lifestyle—has continued. But the teaching of all extant Christian writings up to the time of Constantine is clear. Every extant Christian author who discusses killing forbids it.

What do the historical facts about the early church mean for our question about whether Christians should ever kill? It certainly does not settle the question for us today. Jesus and the Scriptures, not the early fathers, are our final authority. But the Christians of the second and third centuries were much closer to Jesus and the writers of the New Testament than we are. They read the New Testament in the same language in which it was written. Their world was substantially closer to the world of Jesus than is ours. It is not unreasonable to conclude that they had at least as good and perhaps a better understanding of what Jesus meant than Christians living two thousand years later.

CONSTANTINIAN CHRISTIANITY AND KILLING

When Constantine issued the decree in AD 313 that made it legal to be a Christian, Christians entered a dramatically new period of history. It is hardly surprising that Christians cheered Constantine's military victories. Vastly more Christians joined the Roman army, and within one hundred years, *only* Christians could serve in the Roman army.

In the one hundred years after Constantine, leading Christian theologians—especially Ambrose (about 340–397), bishop of Milan, and Augustine (354–430), bishop of Hippo in North Africa—developed the basic framework of the just war tradition. In the subsequent centuries, Christian thinkers refined and developed the just war criteria. From the fifth century to the present, the just war tradition has been the "official" position of most Christians.

During the Middle Ages, Christian theologians and leaders continued to reflect on and seek to apply the tradition. There were some efforts to reduce war. Unfortunately, the church itself launched the Crusades as a holy war willed by Christ to capture and free the Holy Land from centuries of Muslim control. Christ was summoning Christians, prominent church leaders proclaimed, to slaughter the infidels controlling the Holy Land.

There was a very small pacifist tradition in the Middle Ages. But it existed only among fringe Christian groups.

THE REFORMATION

The mainstream Protestant Reformers—Lutheran, Calvinist, and Anglican—affirmed and taught the just war tradition as the proper Christian understanding of war. They also incorporated it into their official creeds, thus declaring it to be Christian orthodoxy.

ANABAPTISTS

The Anabaptists disagreed. Jesus, they insisted, taught his disciples never to kill. The Anabaptists also rejected the union of church and state. Thus they abandoned two central pieces of Christian life (the state church and the just war tradition) that had prevailed for over a thousand years. All other Christians were furious. And they all—Catholics, Lutherans, Anglicans, Zwinglians, and Calvinists—executed the new "heretics." Anabaptists died by the hundreds.

They survived by fleeing to remote places and occasionally finding a tolerant prince. Again and again, they emigrated to places around the world where rulers tolerated their refusal to participate in war. Now known as Mennonites, they have especially flourished in North America, where they are recognized as one of the major denominations in the historic peace church tradition.

QUAKERS

The Quakers emerged out of the Puritan party in the civil wars in England, in the middle of the seventeenth century. Moved by powerful personal religious experiences and their reading of the New Testament, the Quakers (also called Friends) became a vigorous pacifist voice in late seventeenth-century England.

The opportunity for an amazing experiment in nonviolence emerged when the king of England repaid a debt to the father of the young Quaker nobleman, William Penn (1644–1718). The king gave Penn a large tract of land in America, called Pennsylvania. As the first governor, Penn set out to establish peaceful, just relations with the Native Americans living in his colony. The result was probably the best historical example of fair treatment of Native Americans by Europeans. Peace with the Native Americans lasted for about seventy-five years (from 1682 to 1756). Quakers, who controlled the colony's legislature, refused to vote for military expenditures until 1756. But when the French and Indian War broke out in 1756, the Quaker majority in the Pennsylvania legislature reluctantly voted to fund the military campaign. Then, after intense internal discussion in Quaker circles, the Quakers simply refused to run as candidates in the next election. Nonpacifists took over the legislature. But Quakers continue to the present as an important pacifist voice in the United States and around the world.

EARLY HOLINESS AND PENTECOSTAL DENOMINATIONS

Several evangelical denominations and a majority of Pentecostal denominations embraced pacifism in their early years. In fact, thirteen of twenty-one (62 percent) Pentecostal groups formed by 1917 give evidence of being pacifist at some point. The same is true of 50 percent of those groups formed by 1934.

WESLEYAN METHODISTS

The official Discipline of the Wesleyan Methodist Connection declared in 1844: "We believe the Gospel of Christ to be every way opposed to the practice of war." But when the Civil War broke out, their opposition to slavery led them to support the North in the war.

CHURCH OF GOD (ANDERSON)

Quakers and Mennonites were active in some of the movements that led to the emergence of Holiness denominations in the latter part of the nineteenth century. That was certainly true of the Church of God (Anderson), which emerged in Indiana around 1880. A declaration signed by top leaders of the church declared that it was contrary to their religious convictions as followers of Christ to take human life. By the time of World War I, this group had officially registered with the U.S. government as claiming exemption from the draft because of long-held religious convictions. But many church members joined the army. Then in 1932, the general ministerial assembly of the church declared: "We will never again sanction or participate in any war." But again in World War II, a majority of church members who were drafted joined the U.S. Army.

CHURCHES OF CHRIST

In the first half of the nineteenth century, Alexander Campbell was the most prominent leader in the formation of a restorationist movement, called the Disciples of Christ. Campbell himself was an absolute pacifist. Later in the nineteenth century, a church split led to the formation of the Churches of Christ, which continued to be pacifist until 1917.

ASSEMBLIES OF GOD

Started in 1914, the Assemblies of God today is the largest Pentecostal denomination, with approximately 50 million adherents around the world. In 1917, the General Council of the Assemblies of God issued a strong pacifist statement. Citing a number of biblical statements, including Jesus' "Love your enemies," they declared: "We cannot conscientiously participate in war and armed resistance which involves the actual destruction of human life, since this is contrary to our view of the clear teachings of the inspired Word of God." This statement was the official position of the Assemblies of God until 1967.

CHURCH OF GOD (CLEVELAND, TENNESSEE)

Another one of the larger Pentecostal denominations, the Church of God (Cleveland, Tennessee) emerged in the early twentieth century. The founder, Ambrose Jessup Tomlinson, was a strong pacifist. In 1917, Tomlinson wrote that if any church members advocated war or joining the military, they would be considered disloyal to the church and subject to expulsion. And the "Teachings" document of the church in 1917 said simply: "Against members going to war."[4] The church remained pacifist until 1945.

CHURCH OF GOD IN CHRIST (COGIC)

With more than six million members in the United States, COGIC is the largest African American Pentecostal denomination. It was founded in 1895 by Bishop C. H. Mason, COGIC's first General Overseer. Mason repeatedly stated in official documents that the creed of the church had always been that church members are "not allowed to carry arms or to shed the blood of any man and still be members of said church." Until today, the church's official position remains opposed to Christians participating in war.

PROMINENT INDIVIDUAL PACIFISTS IN THE PAST TWO HUNDRED YEARS

Some famous people, including Martin Luther King Jr. and Dorothy Day, are widely known as people who espoused nonviolence. The pacifist commitments of other famous people, like Dwight L. Moody and Charles Spurgeon, are not so well known.

Dwight L. Moody was one of the most famous evangelists in the late nineteenth century. He was also a lifelong pacifist.

Catherine Booth, cofounder of the Salvation Army, and her son Herbert Booth were both pacifists. Charles Haddon Spurgeon (1834–92), a theological conservative, was one of the most popular preachers of his day. His vast number of sermons and commentaries are still quite widely read today. He was also a pacifist.

William Lloyd Garrison (1805–79), one of the most prominent American abolitionists, was a pacifist all his life. Garrison grew up in a Baptist home and knew the Bible thoroughly, but later in life he rejected orthodox Christianity. Garrison was a key leader of the pacifist New England Non-Resistance Society (1838–50), and many of its members were evangelicals.

William Jennings Bryan (1860–1925), theological conservative, prominent presidential candidate, and then Secretary of State under President Wilson, was a pacifist and admirer of Leo Tolstoy for a number of years. John Stott, perhaps the second most influential evangelical after Billy Graham in the second half of the twentieth century, became a pacifist as a young Christian. Later, however, Stott resigned from a pacifist society and embraced a just war stance. Evangelical scholar Ben Witherington, professor of New Testament at Asbury Theological Seminary and author of dozens of books, is a pacifist. So is widely read evangelical scholar Scot McKnight.

There were, of course, many other famous Christian pacifists in the twentieth century: Archbishop Desmond Tutu of South Africa; Archbishop Dom Hélder Câmara of Brazil; Nobel prize winner Adolfo Pérez Esquivel of Argentina; and Stanley Hauerwas, one of the most influential Christian ethicists in the past forty years. Many members of the Catholic organization Pax Christi International (co-led for many years by Marie Dennis) have been pacifists.

NUCLEAR PACIFISM

As both the Soviet Union and the United States developed large numbers of nuclear weapons in the decades after World War II, a number of prominent just war Christians (including John Stott) became nuclear pacifists. To the issue of nuclear war, they applied the just war criteria of just intention (the intent must be the restoration of justice, not revenge), reasonable hope of success, and noncombatant immunity. Their conclusion? They must be nuclear pacifists.

Many Christians (including the U.S. Catholic bishops) argued that the just war criteria would not allow any *use* of nuclear weapons. But they did accept the continued temporary *possession* of nuclear weapons.

On the other hand, many prominent Christian leaders in the just war tradition rejected even the possession of nuclear weapons. In 1978, a number of Christians signed "A Call to Faithfulness" and pledged not to cooperate with the U.S. government's preparations for nuclear war. "On all levels—research, development, testing, production, deployment, and actual use of nuclear weapons—we commit ourselves to resist in the name of Jesus." Those signing this document included not only prominent mainline Protestants and Catholics but also well-known evangelicals: Jay Kesler, president of Youth for Christ; Frank Gaebelein, former coeditor of *Christianity Today*; and Vernon Grounds, longtime president of Conservative Baptist Theological Seminary.

GROWING CATHOLIC AFFIRMATION OF PACIFISM

The Catholic Church's attitude toward pacifism has changed substantially since World War II. In 1956, Pope Pius XII said pacifism was unacceptable as a moral posture. But in the next few decades, the pope and bishops endorsed pacifism as an equally valid Catholic stance alongside the just war position.

In 1965, the encyclical Pastoral Constitution on the Church in the Modern World (*Gaudium et Spes*) stated its intention "to undertake an evaluation of war with an entirely new attitude." The result was praise for pacifism.

There had been individual Catholic pacifists, but *Gaudium et Spes* was quite different. This was an official recognition of the legitimacy of pacifism at the highest level of the Catholic Church. As a result, in their pastoral letter of 1983, *The Challenge of Peace*, the U.S. Catholic bishops recognized the validity of two Catholic positions on war: "The 'new moment' in which we find ourselves sees the just war teaching and nonviolence as distinct but interdependent methods of evaluating warfare." The importance of this statement is underlined by the fact that it is part of an extensive positive discussion of pacifist nonviolence, with mention of pacifism in the early church and modern pacifists like Dorothy Day and Martin Luther King Jr.

In his 1991 encyclical *Centesimus Annus*, Pope John Paul II celebrated the fact that the defeat of the communist dictatorships in eastern Europe in 1989 was accomplished largely by peaceful protest. And Pope John Paul II concluded: "I pray that this example will prevail in other places and other circumstances. May people learn to fight for justice without violence." The official Catechism of the Catholic Church also affirms pacifism. In 2007, Pope Benedict XVI declared that Jesus' command "Love your enemies" is "the *magna carta* of Christian nonviolence." Indeed, the pope said, "Love of one's enemy constitutes the nucleus of the 'Christian revolution.'"

Clearly, official contemporary Catholic teaching not only encourages much greater use of nonviolent methods; it also affirms, in ways that it has not for 1,500 years, that pacifism is a valid, significant Christian stance.

Many Christians today are pacifists. Perhaps today more than at any time since the three centuries before Constantine, significant numbers of Christians believe that Jesus calls them to refuse to kill their enemies.

QUESTIONS FOR REFLECTION AND DISCUSSION

1. What do we know about the early church's attitude toward killing in the years before Emperor Constantine?

2. What does the teaching of the early church mean for our thinking today?

3. How did the church's views on killing change after Emperor Constantine? Why do you think that happened?

4. How does your church relate to the different views on killing in the Reformation?

5. What do you and your friends know about and think about Quaker pacifism?

6. Were you surprised at the fact that many early Pentecostal and some evangelical denominations were originally pacifist? Why?

7. What evidence is there that in more recent years, pacifism has emerged as a more substantial option for Christians? Is that important? If so, why?

14

If Jesus Is Lord

AT THE CENTER of historic Christian faith is the belief that the teacher of love from Nazareth is true God as well as true man. If one accepts that teaching of the church for two millennia, one must embrace and seek to live Jesus' ethical teaching. For every person who affirms historic Christian orthodoxy, the most important question for our topic is clearly this: What did Jesus tell us about killing our enemies?

The historical record is clear. Jesus of Nazareth lived at a time when violent Jewish rebels frequently urged their people to take up arms against the oppressing Roman imperialists. In Jesus' day, there was widespread expectation among the Jewish people that a military messiah would appear to drive out the Romans in a violent military victory. The Jewish historian Josephus reports a number of violent Jewish rebellions against Rome in the decades before and after the lifetime of Jesus. Josephus also reports that this Jewish messianic expectation eventually led to the Jewish War against Rome (AD 66–70) and the total destruction of Jerusalem.

Indirectly at first, but then clearly, Jesus claimed to be that long-expected Messiah. He said the messianic kingdom of justice and peace was actually arriving in his own person and work. But Jesus dramatically redefined the messianic role. He said that in the new dawning kingdom, his followers must love their enemies, not kill them, as the violent Jewish revolutionaries demanded. He repeatedly told his followers that (contrary to every contemporary messianic expectation) he would accomplish his mission by submitting to Roman crucifixion. In his clearest public messianic claim, he rode into Jerusalem, not on a military conqueror's warhorse, but on a humble donkey. On the cross, he lived his call to love one's enemies, asking God to forgive those who crucified him.

Matthew clearly presents the Sermon on the Mount as Jesus' teaching on how he expects his followers to live in the dawning messianic kingdom. His followers must reject the central principle of Old Testament jurisprudence (an "eye for an eye") and instead respond with love (although not passively) to oppressors. That even includes responding to Roman soldiers, who are enforcing imperialist oppression, by offering to carry their packs not just the legally mandated one mile but even a second mile. In fact, Jesus gave the unprecedented command to his followers to love their enemies—a teaching contrary to the practice of virtually every human society that has ever existed.

Rejecting the narrow nationalism of much Jewish messianic expectation, Jesus said his kingdom was for everyone: despised Samaritans, sinners of all sorts, even oppressive Romans. "I say to you that many will come from the east and the west, and will take their places at the feast with Abraham, Isaac and Jacob in the kingdom of heaven" (Matthew 8:11).

Both Jewish and Roman leaders decided that Jesus' radical messianic claims and teaching were a threat to their power. So they arranged his crucifixion. The implications for Jesus' followers were painfully obvious. Every Jew in Jesus' day knew that anyone who claimed to be the expected messiah and then was crucified was a fraud. There is absolutely no evidence of followers of a messianic claimant continuing to believe in that leader after his opponents killed him. For Jews of Jesus' day, there was only one conclusion on the day after the crucifixion: Jesus was a fake, a fraud, and his movement was finished. Nothing short of meeting the resurrected Jesus could have convinced his discouraged disciples that Jesus' messianic proclamation was still true and that they should now tell the world that his peaceful kingdom had truly broken into history.

There is evidence throughout the rest of the New Testament that the early church understood and embraced Jesus' message of peace. The word translated "peace" (*eirēnē*) appears ninety-nine times in the New Testament. Peter and Paul sometimes use the word translated "peace" to sum up the whole Christian message. Peter learns, in his encounter with Cornelius, that Jesus' peaceful kingdom even includes Roman imperialists, the national enemies of the Jews. Ephesians explains that the overcoming of the worst ethnic prejudice and hostility at that time in history is central to Jesus' gospel of peace. We see in the epistles, especially clearly in Romans (12:14-21), echoes of Jesus' rejection of retaliation, such as an eye for an eye. Frequently New Testament writers command Christians to imitate Christ at the cross, where he loved even his enemies. And from the writings of Christians up until the time of Constantine, we know that the early church's teachers taught that Jesus intended for his followers never to kill anyone. Every extant writing by

Christians (up until Constantine) that discusses the topic of killing says clearly that Christians should never kill, whether in abortion, capital punishment, or war.

The most profound theological foundation for the conviction that Christians should love their enemies, not kill their enemies, is the cross. In the Sermon on the Mount, Jesus taught that his followers should love their enemies because that is what God does. And the apostle Paul wrote that at the cross, Christ died for *sinful enemies*! We will never fathom the full mystery, but Christians believe that the trinitarian God—Father, Son, and Holy Spirit—suffered the agony of Roman crucifixion. God somehow took our sins upon Godself to accomplish the forgiveness and reconciliation of God's enemies. Since that is the way God treats God's enemies, Christ's followers must treat their enemies in the same way.

It is interesting that no one states this more clearly than the prominent just war advocate Paul Ramsey. After saying that for almost two centuries, the early Christians "were universally pacifists," Ramsey explains their pacifism with the comment: "How could anyone, who knew himself to be classed with transgressors and the enemies of God whom Christ came to die to save, love his own life and seek to save it more than that of his own enemy or murderer?"[1] That ethical-theological conclusion, it seems to me, remains as true today as in the second and third centuries.

The evidence of the New Testament is quite clear: Jesus called his followers to love their enemies, not kill them. One can conclude, with people like Reinhold Niebuhr, that while that is what Jesus taught, it does not work in the real world. From that perspective, we should ignore what Jesus taught. But that option is simply not available to anyone with an orthodox understanding of who Jesus is. If Jesus is true God as well as true man, then it is profoundly heretical to say that Jesus' followers should reject one of his central teachings. Evangelicals and other historically orthodox Christians simply dare not do that.

If Jesus is God incarnate; if Jesus truly was the expected Messiah, the Christ; if Jesus taught his followers to love, not kill their enemies; if Jesus' messianic kingdom has begun in his life, death, and resurrection; if the church, in the power of the Holy Spirit, is called to live now the lifestyle of the already dawning kingdom modeled by Jesus; and if the crucified and risen Jesus is *now* Lord of all earthly kingdoms: then Christians today must refuse to kill their enemies. Miroslav Volf is right: "If one decides to put on soldier's gear instead of carrying one's cross, one should not seek legitimation in the religion that worships the crucified Messiah."[2]

QUESTIONS FOR REFLECTION AND DISCUSSION

1. Do you agree that the most important question on this topic is, What did Jesus teach about killing? Why?

2. Do most Christians you know make this the most import-ant question? If not, why not?

3. How many of the affirmations in the last paragraph do you agree with? How many of these affirmations do most Christians agree with?

4. Take some time to ponder your final answer to the basic question, What did Jesus teach on killing? How has your answer shaped your life up to the present? How do you want it to shape your life in the future?

Notes

ACKNOWLEDGMENTS

1 For details, see the entire January 2015 issue of the *Mennonite Quarterly Review*, especially Rachel Waltner Goossen, "Defanging the Beast: Mennonite Responses to John Howard Yoder's Sexual Abuse," 7–80, http://www.bishop-accountability.org/news5/2015_01_Goossen_Defanging_the_Beast.pdf.

1 THE CENTRAL QUESTIONS

1 C. S. Lewis, *The Weight of Glory* (San Francisco: HarperCollins, 2001), 86. From a 1940 speech, "Why I Am Not a Pacifist," to a pacifist society at Oxford University.
2 For more examples, see Ronald J. Sider, *Nonviolent Action: What Christian Ethics Demands but Most Christians Have Never Really Tried* (Grand Rapids, MI: Brazos, 2015).
3 Erica Chenoweth and Maria J. Stephan, *Why Civil Resistance Works: The Strategic Logic of Nonviolent Conflict* (New York: Columbia University Press, 2011), 7.

2 THE SETTING FOR JESUS' RADICAL TEACHING

1 Palestinian Targum on Genesis 48:10; quoted in Martin Hengel, *Victory over Violence*, trans. David E. Green (London: SPCK, 1975), 69.

2 Craig S. Keener, *A Commentary on the Gospel of Matthew* (Grand Rapids, MI: Eerdmans, 1999), 168.

3 N. T. Wright, *The New Testament and the People of God* (Minneapolis: Fortress Press, 1992), 176.

4 Wright, *New Testament and the People of God*, 173.

5 N. T. Wright, *Jesus and the Victory of God* (Minneapolis: Fortress Press, 1996), 204.

6 Wright, *Jesus and the Victory of God*, 465.

7 Richard Hays, *The Moral Vision of the New Testament* (San Francisco: HarperSanFrancisco, 1996), 321.

8 See Aida Besancon Spencer, "Jesus' Treatment of Women in the Gospels," in *Discovering Biblical Equality*, ed. Ronald W. Pierce and Rebecca Merrill Groothuis (Downers Grove, IL: InterVarsity Press, 2004), 126–41.

9 Wright, *Jesus and the Victory of God*, 604.

10 Wright, *Jesus and the Victory of God*, 564.

11 Lisa Sharon Harper, *The Very Good Gospel: How Everything Wrong Can Be Made Right* (New York: WaterBrook, 2016), 6.

3 LIVING IN JESUS' DAWNING KINGDOM

1 R. T. France, *Gospel of Matthew* (Grand Rapids, MI: Eerdmans, 2007), 187.

2 Joachim Jeremias, *Jerusalem in the Time of Jesus* (Philadelphia: Fortress Press, 1975), 376.

3 Luke 6:29-31 also has this statement with some modest variations.

4 N. T. Wright, *Jesus and the Victory of God* (Minneapolis: Fortress Press, 1996), 291.

5 See Walter Wink, *Engaging the Powers: Discernment and Resistance in a World of Domination* (Minneapolis: Fortress Press, 1992), 175–84. A number of scholars agree with Wink's interpretation. See David P. Gushee and Glen H. Stassen, *Kingdom Ethics: Following Jesus in Contemporary Context* (Downers Grove, IL: InterVarsity Press, 2003), 139; Thomas R. Yoder Neufeld, *Killing Enmity: Violence and*

the New Testament (Grand Rapids, MI: Baker Academic, 2011), 23–25.

6 The words are *chitōn*, meaning the inner garment worn next to the skin, and *himation*, meaning the outer garment; as defined in H. G. Liddell and R. Scott, *A Greek Lexicon*, 9th ed. (Oxford: Clarendon, 1958), 829.

7 Wink, *Engaging the Powers*, 182.

8 Richard Hays, *The Moral Vision of the New Testament: A Contemporary Introduction to New Testament Ethics* (San Francisco: HarperSanFrancisco, 1996), 328.

9 Quoted in William Klassen, "'Love Your Enemies': Some Reflections on the Current Status of Research," in *The Love of Enemy and Nonretaliation in the New Testament*, ed. Willard Swartley (Louisville: Westminster John Knox, 1992), 11. So too Wolfgang Schrage, *The Ethics of the New Testament* (Philadelphia: Fortress Press, 1988), 76.

10 Martin Hengel, *Christ and Power* (Philadelphia: Fortress Press, 1977), 19.

11 Martin Hengel, *Was Jesus a Revolutionist?* (Philadelphia: Fortress Press, 1971), 26–27.

12 Ronald J. Sider, ed., *The Early Church on Killing: A Comprehensive Sourcebook on War, Abortion, and Capital Punishment* (Grand Rapids, MI: Baker Academic, 2012), 171–72.

4 FURTHER CLAIMS OF JESUS AND HOW CHRISTIANS EVADE THEM

1 N. T. Wright, *Jesus and the Victory of God* (Minneapolis: Fortress Press, 1996), 40, 81, 95–96; and Wright, *The New Testament and the People of God* (Minneapolis: Fortress Press, 1992), 333–34.

2 Eduard Schweizer, *The Good News According to Matthew* (Atlanta: John Knox Press, 1975), 194.

3 Ronald J. Sider, ed., *The Early Church on Killing: A Comprehensive Sourcebook on War, Abortion, and Capital Punishment* (Grand Rapids, MI: Baker Academic, 2012), 165–95. For abortion, see 165–66; for infanticide, 110–11; for capital punishment, 166–68; for war and military service, 168–90.

4 Sider, *The Early Church on Killing*, 110.

5 Origen, *Against Celsus* 4.9; 7.26. Sider, *The Early Church on Killing*, 73, 76.

5 DOES THE REST OF THE NEW TESTAMENT REFLECT WHAT JESUS TAUGHT?

1   Ulrich Mauser, *The Gospel of Peace* (Louisville: Westminster John Knox Press, 1992), 106.
2   See the rather similar statement in Colossians 1:26-27.
3   Mauser, *The Gospel of Peace*, 186.
4   See further Ronald J. Sider, *Just Politics: A Guide for Christian Engagement* (Grand Rapids, MI: Brazos, 2012), 50–51, and the literature cited in notes 36–42.
5   See Colossians 3:13; 1 John 2:6; Romans 6:6-11; 2 Corinthians 8:9; Galatians 2:20; Ephesians 4:20-24; Colossians 2:12-13.
6   John 13:1-17; Romans 15:1-7; 2 Corinthians 5:14-21.

6 BUT WHAT ABOUT . . . ?

1   F. F. Bruce, *Romans* (Grand Rapids, MI: Eerdmans, 1963), 238.
2   Ben Witherington III, *The Paul Quest* (Downers Grove, IL: Inter-Varsity Press, 1998), 178.
3   Miroslav Volf, *Exclusion and Embrace* (Nashville: Abingdon, 1996), 302, 304.
4   Friedrich Nietzsche, *"The Birth of Tragedy" and "The Genealogy of Morals,"* trans. Francis Golffing (Garden City: Doubleday, 1956), 185; quoted in Richard Hays, *The Moral Vision of the New Testament* (San Francisco: HarperSanFrancisco, 1996), 169.
5   For a discussion of the use of symbolic language in apocalyptic literature, see Gregory A. Boyd, *The Crucifixion of the Warrior God* (Minneapolis: Fortress Press, 2017), 597–601, and the literature cited there.

7 JESUS AND KILLING IN THE OLD TESTAMENT

1   Eric A. Seibert, *The Violence of Scripture: Overcoming the Old Testament's Troubling Legacy* (Minneapolis: Fortress Press, 2012), 86
2   See the book-length analysis of Yoder's understanding of the Old Testament, John C. Nugent, *The Politics of Yahweh: John Howard Yoder, The Old Testament, and the People of God* (Eugene, OR: Cascade Books, 2011). Nugent describes Yoder's approach as "canonical-directional" (11).
3   John Howard Yoder, *The Original Revolution: Essays on Christian Pacifism* (Scottdale, PA: Herald Press, 1971), 104–7.
4   Nugent, *Politics of Yahweh*, 112–13.

5   Gregory A. Boyd, *Crucifixion of the Warrior God* (Minneapolis: Fortress Press, 2017).

6   It is impossible to adequately summarize his many extensive exegetical and theological arguments in a few paragraphs!

8 FOUNDATIONAL THEOLOGICAL ISSUES

1   For an exhaustive discussion of the historical evidence for Jesus' resurrection, see N. T. Wright, *The Resurrection of the Son of God* (Minneapolis: Fortress Press, 2002); and Michael R. Licona, *The Resurrection of Jesus: A New Historiographical Approach* (Downers Grove, IL: InterVarsity Press Academic, 2010).

2   N. T. Wright, *Surprised by Hope: Rethinking Heaven, the Resurrection, and the Mission of the Church* (New York: HarperOne, 2008), 209.

3   Lisa Sowle Cahill, *Love Your Enemies: Discipleship, Pacifism, and Just War Theory* (Minneapolis: Fortress Press, 1994), 79, 213.

4   See Ronald J. Sider, *The Scandal of the Evangelical Conscience: Why Are Christians Living Just Like the Rest of the World?* (Grand Rapids, MI: Baker Books, 2005), 31–53.

9 PROBLEMS WITH PACIFISM

1   Erica Chenoweth and Maria J. Stephan, *Why Civilian Resistance Works: The Strategic Logic of Nonviolent Conflict* (New York: Columbia University Press, 2011), 7.

2   J. Daryl Charles and Timothy J. Demy, *War, Peace, and Christianity: Questions and Answers from a Just-War Perspective* (Wheaton, IL: Crossway, 2010), 145.

3   Oliver O'Donovan, *The Just War Revisited* (Cambridge: Cambridge University Press, 2003), 7–8.

4   Duane K. Friesen, *Christian Peacemaking and International Conflict* (Scottdale, PA: Herald Press, 1986), 42.

10 PROBLEMS WITH JUST WAR THINKING

1   Quoted in Gregory A. Boyd, *Crucifixion of the Warrior God* (2 vols; Minneapolis: Fortress, 2017), I,291.

11 WHAT IF MOST (OR ALL) CHRISTIANS BECAME PACIFISTS?

1   See Ronald J. Sider, *Nonviolent Action: What Christian Ethics Demands But Most Christians Have Never Really Tried* (Grand Rapids, MI: Brazos Press, 2015).

2   Cited in Sider, *Nonviolent Action*, 74.

12 NONVIOLENCE AND THE ATONEMENT

1   J. Denny Weaver, *The Nonviolent Atonement*, 2nd ed. (Grand Rapids, MI: Eerdmans, 2011), 245, with his emphasis.

2   Sharon L. Baker, *Razing Hell: Rethinking Everything You've Been Taught about God's Wrath and Judgment* (Louisville: Westminster John Knox Press, 2010), 35. See also Baker, *Executing God: Rethinking Everything You've Been Taught about Salvation and the Cross* (Louisville: Westminster John Knox Press, 2013), 70–78.

3   Weaver, *The Nonviolent Atonement*, 89, 245–46.

4   See Joanna Carlson Brown and Rebecca Parker, "For God So Loved the World?" in *Christianity, Patriarchy, and Abuse: A Feminist Critique*, eds. Joanne Carlson Brown and Carole R. Bohn (New York: Pilgrim, 1989), 1–30.

5   C. H. Dodd, *The Epistle of Paul to the Romans* (London: Hodder and Stoughton, 1932), 23.

6   And Christ's battle with the demons during his public ministry. See Ronald J. Sider, *Good News and Good Works: A Theology for the Whole Gospel* (Grand Rapids, MI: Baker Books, 1999), 97–98.

7   Mary H. Schertz, "Partners in God's Passion," in *At Peace and Unafraid: Public Order, Security, and the Wisdom of the Cross*, ed. Duane K. Friesen and Gerald W. Schlabach (Scottdale, PA: Herald Press, 2005), 173.

8   This section includes material from Sider, *Good News and Good Works*, 95–100.

9   Scot McKnight, *A Community Called Atonement* (Nashville: Abingdon, 2007), 11.

13 CHRISTIANS AND KILLING IN CHURCH HISTORY

1   Peter J. Leithart, *Defending Constantine* (Downers Grove, IL: InterVarsity Press Academic, 2010), 278.

2   Ronald J. Sider, *The Early Church on Killing: A Comprehensive Sourcebook on War, Abortion, and Capital Punishment* (Grand Rapids,

MI: Baker Academic, 2012).

3 Sider, *The Early Church on Killing*, 110.

4 Jay Beaman and Brian K. Pipkin, eds., *Pentecostal and Holiness Statements on War and Peace* (Eugene, OR: Pickwick Publications, 2013), 152–53.

14 IF JESUS IS LORD

1 Paul Ramsey, *War and the Christian Conscience* (Durham, NC: Duke University Press, 1961), xv, xvi.

2 Miroslav Volf, *Exclusion and Embrace: A Theological Exploration of Identity, Otherness, and Reconciliation* (Nashville: Abingdon, 1996), 306.

The Author

RONALD J. SIDER is the author or editor of forty books, including *Rich Christians in an Age of Hunger*, and is internationally renowned for his leadership among Christians who recognize the social, political, and spiritual implications of the gospel. Having earned a PhD from Yale University, Sider is distinguished senior professor emeritus of theology, holistic ministry, and public policy at Palmer Seminary at Eastern University and is founder and president emeritus of Evangelicals for Social Action. An ordained minister in both Mennonite and Brethren in Christ denominations, Sider lives with his wife, Arbutus, in eastern Pennsylvania. He blogs at RonSiderBlog.substack.com.